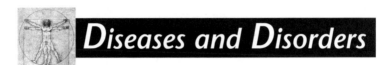

Diseases and Disorders

Alzheimer's Disease

Titles in the Diseases and Disorders series include:

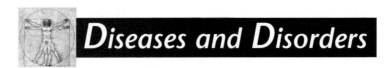
Diseases and Disorders

Alzheimer's Disease

by Linda Jacobs Altman

Library of Congress Cataloging-in-Publication Data

Altman, Linda Jacobs, 1943–
    Alzheimer's disease / by Linda Jacobs Altman.
    p. cm. — (Diseases and disorders series)
    Includes bibliographical references and index.
    Summary: Discusses Alzheimer's disease including
its history, how it assaults the brain, its diagnosis,
its treatment, and its future.
    ISBN 1-56006-695-4 (hardcover : alk. paper)
    1. Alzheimer's disease—Juvenile literature.
[1. Alzheimer's disease. 2. Diseases.] I. Title. II. Series.
    RC523 .A366   2001
    616.8'31—dc21   00-009237

Copyright © 2001 by Lucent Books, Inc.
P.O. Box 289011
San Diego, CA 92198-9011
Printed in the U.S.A.

Table of Contents

"The Most Difficult Puzzles Ever Devised"

CHARLES BEST, ONE of the pioneers in the search for a cure for diabetes, once explained what it is about medical research that intrigued him so. "It's not just the gratification of knowing one is helping people," he confided, "although that probably is a more heroic and selfless motivation. Those feelings may enter in, but truly, what I find best is the feeling of going toe to toe with nature, of trying to solve the most difficult puzzles ever devised. The answers are there somewhere, those keys that will solve the puzzle and make the patient well. But how will those keys be found?"

Since the dawn of civilization, nothing has so puzzled people—and often frightened them, as well—as the onset of illness in a body or mind that had seemed healthy before. A seizure, the inability of a heart to pump, the sudden deterioration of muscle tone in a small child—being unable to reverse such conditions or even to understand why they occur was unspeakably frustrating to healers. Even before there were names for such conditions, even before they were understood at all, each was a reminder of how complex the human body was, and how vulnerable.

While our grappling with understanding diseases has been frustrating at times, it has also provided some of humankind's most heroic accomplishments. Alexander Fleming's accidental discovery in 1928 of a mold that could be turned into penicillin

6

has resulted in the saving of untold millions of lives. The isolation of the enzyme insulin has reversed what was once a death sentence for anyone with diabetes. There have been great strides in combating conditions for which there is not yet a cure, too. Medicines can help AIDS patients live longer, diagnostic tools such as mammography and ultrasound can help doctors find tumors while they are treatable, and laser surgery techniques have made the most intricate, minute operations routine.

This "toe-to-toe" competition with diseases and disorders is even more remarkable when seen in a historical continuum. An astonishing amount of progress has been made in a very short time. Just two hundred years ago, the existence of germs as a cause of some diseases was unknown. In fact, it was less than 150 years ago that a British surgeon named Joseph Lister had difficulty persuading his fellow doctors that washing their hands before delivering a baby might increase the chances of a healthy delivery (especially if they had just attended to a diseased patient)!

Each book in Lucent's *Diseases and Disorders* series explores a disease or disorder and the knowledge that has been accumulated (or discarded) by doctors through the years. Each book also examines the tools used for pinpointing a diagnosis, as well as the various means that are used to treat or cure a disease. Finally, new ideas are presented—techniques or medicines that may be on the horizon.

Frustration and disappointment are still part of medicine, for not every disease or condition can be cured or prevented. But the limitations of knowledge are being pushed outward constantly; the "most difficult puzzles ever devised" are finding challengers every day.

The Thief of Memory

E LIZABETH P.* SAT at the kitchen table, with her checkbook and bank statement in front of her. She had balanced her statement every month for more than fifty years. Now she stared blankly at the jumble of papers, wondering exactly what she was supposed to do with them. Elizabeth broke down crying.

A neighbor found her like that, crying over papers she could no longer understand. It must be her eyes, the neighbor said.

That made sense to Elizabeth. It had been a long time since she last visited the optometrist. She probably needed new glasses.

Elizabeth got her new glasses, but the bank statement remained a mystery. So did many other things: names, dates, common tasks like making coffee or vacuuming the living room rug. Elizabeth P. had Alzheimer's disease.

Defining Alzheimer's Disease

Alzheimer's is a form of dementia, or the loss of intellectual function. It destroys memory and judgment and produces often-frightening changes in behavior. People who were gentle may become combative. Those who had a good sense of humor may become morose and suspicious.

Patients also become increasingly helpless, as they forget how to do the ordinary tasks of daily living. Simple things like getting dressed, brushing teeth, or taking a bath become confusing impossibilities.

---

* Elizabeth's last name has been omitted to preserve her family's privacy.

Alzheimer's disease is called the thief of memory because it gradually destroys the memory of its victims.

Alzheimer's disease has been called many things: the thief of memory, the living death, the long goodbye. It well deserves this fearsome reputation. In stealing mind and memory, it steals the self. For an extra measure of misery, Alzheimer's disease does its work slowly. Victims can live for five or ten years or even longer, becoming progressively worse as time passes.

There is no cure for Alzheimer's disease, and no way to prevent it. Scientists aren't even sure what causes the characteristic brain damage. They are sure of one thing, however: Answers must be found or this terrible disease will disable and eventually kill millions.

The Scope of the Problem

In 1999, more than 4 million older Americans had Alzheimer's. That number is expected to triple by 2020. This is because people are living longer. Although Alzheimer's does strike middle-aged and even young people, it is primarily a disease of the elderly.

Primarily striking the elderly, Alzheimer's disease afflicts nearly 50 percent of people over the age of eighty-five.

The older the person, the more likely it is that he or she will get the disease.

This likelihood is reflected in U.S. government figures. Studies show that Alzheimer's afflicts one in ten people over the age of sixty-five. It afflicts nearly half of those over eighty-five, a segment of the population that is growing at a stunning rate.

In 1900, only 123,000 people in the United States (0.2 percent of the population) were over the age of eighty-five. By 1990, that number had jumped to 3,021,000 (more than 1 percent). According to Harvard Medical School professor Dr. Muriel Gillick, however, these figures do not adequately express the problem:

> If we [measure by] the fraction of the elderly population (all those sixty-five and over) who are at least eighty-five, what we find is that this number began a sharp ascent in 1950 and has been soaring ever since . . . from a constant 4 percent until 1950 to a staggering 24 percent projected by 2050.[1]

If half those people were afflicted with Alzheimer's, it would cause a full-scale national emergency. The disease would drain public resources much as it drains the minds of its victims.

Scientists, government agencies, and private organizations such as the Alzheimer's Association are working to ensure that this does not happen. They are attacking Alzheimer's on all fronts. Some do basic research into causes. Some seek treatments that will cure the disease or at least slow its progress. Others concentrate on managing symptoms in those who are already afflicted.

Alzheimer victims and their families face a grim reality, but their situation is not without hope. There is always the chance that today's laboratory experiment may become tomorrow's breakthrough. It is this hope that keeps the researchers working, looking for answers to the puzzle that is Alzheimer's disease.

Chapter 1

A History of Alzheimer's Disease

I N 1906, GERMAN physician Alois Alzheimer first described the disease that bears his name. For years afterward, however, the general public heard little about it. Not until the latter twentieth century did the name "Alzheimer's disease" become familiar. For this reason, many people think of it as a new disease. But in reality, it "seems to have been around as long as people have lived to be old enough to develop it,"[2] says Dr. Muriel Gillick.

Alzheimer's and Other Dementing Conditions

For most of human history, Alzheimer's disease was confused with other conditions that produce dementia. When Alzheimer's struck relatively young people, it might be labeled insanity, delirium, or even demon possession. In the elderly, though, it was likely to be called senility, and to be regarded as a normal part of the aging process.

Senility is typically defined as severe mental decline resulting from old age. Old people were expected to become forgetful and to lose their ability to think clearly. Even severe impairment was not considered a disease when it occurred in people over sixty-five.

Today, the word *senile* has gone out of favor. Instead, scientists use the term *dementia* to describe the mental confusion, memory loss, disorientation, and intellectual impairment of diseases such as Alzheimer's. Dementia itself is not a disease, however, nor is it part of normal aging. Rather, it is a set of symptoms produced by disease or injury. Alzheimer's disease is one of several forms of dementia that are both permanent and progressive, meaning that they cannot be cured and get worse over time.

Senility and Dementia in History

In a world that regarded senility as a normal part of aging, the elderly were judged by a different standard than younger people. For example, the Greek philosopher Plato believed that a person "'under the influence of old age' could not be held accountable for his crimes."[3]

Some five hundred years after Plato, the Roman physician Galen described old age as a time of imbecility, or stupidity and foolishness. As Dr. Gillick put it, "Aging was essentially a process of drying out and shriveling up."[4] This "shriveling" process affected the mind as surely as the body.

These attitudes toward aging in general and dementia in particular were shaped by the rarity of both. For much of human history, the average life span was thirty years or less. Few people lived long enough to develop age-related problems. Furthermore, those who did survive rarely enjoyed good health. Conditions such as arthritis, poor vision or hearing, and even dental problems could turn the later years into torment. When dementia was added to the mix, the picture became grim indeed.

In such a world, it was not unreasonable to view mental impairment as a normal part

Plato believed older people could not be held accountable for their crimes.

of the aging process. Then, as now, people tended to think that conditions that appeared together were somehow related. Dementia seemed to be as much a part of old age as losing one's hair or having failing eyesight.

The Strange Case of Auguste D.

Like others of his time, Alois Alzheimer regarded senility as a natural product of aging. When he began working at a mental hospital in Frankfurt, Germany, however, he encountered a patient known as Auguste D. who began showing symptoms of dementia at the age of fifty-one. Alzheimer reasoned that this was far too young for senility, and decided another process must be at work.

Dr. Alzheimer was determined to find out about that process. His study of the woman who would become the first person diagnosed with Alzheimer's disease began on November 26, 1901. Journalist Jeremy Laurance quoted from Alzheimer's notes from that session, placing Auguste D.'s responses in italics:

> She sits on a bed with a helpless expression. What is your name? *Auguste.* Last name? *Auguste.* What is your husband's name? *Auguste, I think.* Your husband. *Ah, my husband.* She looks as if she didn't understand the question. Are you married? *To Auguste.* Mrs D? *Yes, yes. Auguste D.* How long have you been here? She seems to be trying to remember. *Three weeks. . . .*

> At lunch she eats cauliflower and pork. Asked what she is eating she answers spinach. When objects are shown to her she does not remember after a short time which have been shown. . . . Asked to write Auguste D. she writes Mrs and forgets the rest. It is necessary to repeat every word.[5]

Auguste D. deteriorated rapidly. She became unable to talk and lost control of her bowels and bladder. Four and a half years after her symptoms began, she died, never having left the Frankfurt hospital where Dr. Alzheimer found her. She was fifty-five years old.

Alois Alzheimer, the German neurologist for whom Alzheimer's disease is named.

Dr. Alzheimer's Discovery

When Alzheimer examined Auguste D.'s brain after her death, he found it to be shrunken. It resembled a withered walnut, dark and dry. Unnaturally wide spaces separated the folds of nerve tissue. Alzheimer had seen brains like this before. Given Auguste D.'s symptoms, he had expected such damage.

When Alzheimer examined tissue samples from the cerebral cortex, the part of the brain where memory and the higher intellectual functions are located, he found something he had not expected. There were microscopic bundles, or tangles, of dead nerve fibers scattered throughout the tissue.

He also found a second abnormality: round, frecklelike deposits that would later become known as plaques. Like tangles, plaques were scattered throughout the cerebral cortex of Auguste D.'s brain. Alzheimer concluded that he had found a new disease, one that afflicted younger people and mimicked "normal" senility in many ways.

Classifying Alzheimer's Disease

In 1910, psychiatrist Emil Kraepelin first used the name "Alzheimer's disease" to describe the malady that killed Auguste D. Although he noted the similarities between Alzheimer's disease and "normal" senility, he decided that the two were not related. Dr. Muriel Gillick explains,

> Kraepelin acknowledged that the . . . findings suggested that Alzheimer had found an "especially severe form of senile imbecility," but then, evidently rebutting his own argument, said this cannot be because the illness Alzheimer described typically began in [a person's] forties. Kraepelin therefore concluded that it would probably turn out that we are dealing with two different conditions—one a true disease, the other a [normal] disintegration related to old age.[6]

As a result of this theory, Alzheimer's disease was first classified as a "presenile dementia," meaning that it struck only younger people. This complete separation between what was called "Alzheimer's disease" or "presenile dementia" and what was called "normal" senility led to a great deal of misdiagnosis. For example, confronted with a fifty-year-old and an eighty-year-old, both with severe dementia, a doctor would diagnose Alzheimer's disease in the younger patient and "normal" senility in the older one, despite the fact that the conditions were, in reality, one and the same.

Dr. Konrad Maurer holds Alois Alzheimer's medical file on Auguste D., the first person diagnosed as having Alzheimer's disease.

Assessing the Evidence

This presumed difference between dementia in the old and dementia in the relatively young led to some odd findings. For example, at the 1936 meeting of the American and Canadian Medical Associations, a doctor presented a case history of a fifty-three-year-old woman with Alzheimer's disease. After she died, the doctor compared her brain with the brains of elderly people who had suffered from dementia. All the brains evidenced the same shriveling, the same plaques and tangles in the cerebral cortex.

Ordinarily, a scientist confronted with such findings would at least suspect that all the patients had suffered from the same condition. In this case, however, the doctor's belief that "senility" and

A segment of an Alzheimer's afflicted brain (right) appears shriveled when compared to a healthy segment.

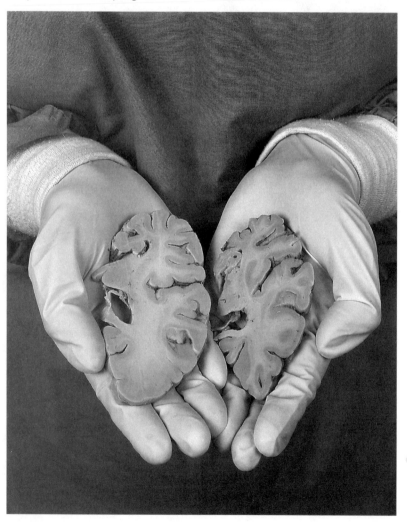

Alzheimer's were different from one another led him to misinterpret his own laboratory evidence. Although the brains looked alike, he concluded that they could not be. As Gillick explained, he "persisted in claiming that the plaques 'somehow differ' and were perhaps more widespread with 'true' Alzheimer's disease."[7]

Such confusion lasted for a long time. In part, this was because early-onset Alzheimer's is rare and therefore more likely to be viewed as abnormal. Although Alzheimer's is not a normal part of the aging process, the majority of victims are in their seventies or eighties. It wasn't until scientists learned more about how the brain ages that they realized dementia is never normal, even in the elderly.

The Aging Brain

In normal aging, the brain slows down, but not nearly as much as was once supposed. Older people often learn more slowly than younger ones, and their reaction times are not as quick. Their memory tends to become selective. Elderly people also often remember the remote past better than they remember recent events. For example, the same woman who can recall the dress she wore to her high school prom fifty years ago may not remember what she wore to a dinner party the week before.

These minor lapses, however, are different from the profound memory loss seen in Alzheimer's disease. In his book *Candle and Darkness*, psychologist Joseph Rogers explains:

Think of your memory as a file cabinet. Every day you put new files in, and every year it gets . . . harder to find any particular file or to stuff a new file into the cabinet. It's normal that we become more forgetful as we grow older. We've got a lot more to remember! But with the Alzheimer's patient, soon something different begins to occur.

At some point, the patients begin to forget very ordinary but important things. Uncle Joe takes his usual afternoon walk in a neighborhood he's lived in for over fifty years, and he can't find his way home.[8]

Alzheimer's victims lose the ability to remember very ordinary, basic things like the names of family members and friends.

The memory loss of Alzheimer's disease is also accompanied by defects in judgment and reasoning. Patients lose the ability to think a problem through, to consider alternatives and arrive at sensible decisions. In normal aging, on the other hand, judgment and reasoning ability decline very little, if at all.

Early Research

The definition of *normal* and *abnormal* varies from culture to culture. Though science is supposed to be unaffected by these distinctions, researchers cannot help bringing their own preconceived notions into the laboratory. What they believe about the world shapes the questions they ask, the experiments they design, and the results they expect to obtain.

Expectations are further shaped by the methods and equipment available to the researchers. For the first half of the twentieth century, scientists simply did not have the tools to study Alzheimer's disease at the molecular level.

Like generations of scientists before them, medical researchers gathered knowledge about disease by studying individual case histories. In clinical, or treatment, settings with actual patients, this meant observing symptoms and charting the progress of the condition. In the laboratory, it meant examining tissue samples for abnormalities that might be related to those symptoms.

Neither type of data, however, provided reliable information about cause and effect because the fact that two conditions appear together does not necessarily mean one caused the other. Drawing such general conclusions from a handful of case histories is considered bad science because there is too much room for error.

New Methods of Research

Medical researchers recognized the limitations of case histories, but they had few alternatives because research with living subjects presents special difficulties. With nonliving subjects, chemists can burn, freeze, irradiate, or otherwise destroy their test samples. Physicists can split atoms and study particles in vacuum chambers in an attempt to understand them. Such procedures are not possible with living human beings.

In the early 1960s, however, new equipment and laboratory methods opened exciting possibilities in medical research. The electron microscope, developed by two German scientists in 1931, had come into general use by the '60s. It could achieve ten times the magnification of conventional microscopes. Aided by this powerful tool, Alzheimer's researchers could see details they

Advances in medical equipment, such as the electron microscope, have helped researchers better understand Alzheimer's disease.

had never seen before. Namely, they could study the structure of plaques and tangles and see how they damaged healthy cells.

In addition to this new technology, medical researchers began using quantitative analysis, or numerical methods, to study great quantities of data. Quantitative analysis had long been one of the standard methods of research in physics and chemistry. By the 1960s, it had become the standard in medical research as well.

Using quantitative analysis, Alzheimer's researchers collected data on how many people in each age group were diagnosed with Alzheimer's. This allowed them to understand the relationship between aging and Alzheimer's in a new way. They could determine which age groups were most at risk for the disease and express that risk as a percentage of the population. For example, they could show that Alzheimer's afflicts 10 percent of those over age sixty-five and nearly half of those over eighty-five.

These new capabilities made it easier for doctors to study dementia. In the mid-1960s, British researchers Martin Roth and Bernard Tomlinson studied brain tissue samples from patients with various types of dementia. They counted plaques and tangles and noted their precise location within each specimen. The experiment confirmed by numerical methods what Alois Alzheimer had determined when he examined Auguste D.'s brain: plaques and tangles concentrated in the parts of the brain that control memory, language, and reasoning.

To the surprise of the British researchers, however, their study showed no significant differences between Alzheimer's disease and senile dementia. Not only were the plaques and tangles identical in structure, they appeared in similar numbers and were distributed in the same areas of the brain. Roth and Tomlinson could not ignore the possibility that Alzheimer's disease and senile dementia were one and the same.

Other studies produced similar results. Scientists set out to find the differences between Alzheimer's disease and senile dementia, only to discover that they could not identify a single one.

By the 1970s, scientists were becoming convinced that there was no reason to distinguish between "presenile" and "senile" forms of dementia. As Gillick said, "Dementia was dementia, regardless of the age of onset. It was a syndrome, a collection of symptoms with a variety of possible causes. The principal cause—whether in people in their fifties and sixties, or in their seventies and eighties—was Alzheimer's disease."[9]

The Prevalence of Alzheimer's Disease

Another surprising discovery came from neurologist Robert Katzman. In the late 1950s, Katzman was studying dementia caused by "normal-pressure hydrocephalus," a condition in which fluid collects in the cavities of the brain. He performed biopsies on patients thought to be suffering from this condition. To his surprise, many of these people did not have normal-pressure hydrocephalus at all. Samples of their brain tissue clearly showed the characteristic plaques and tangles of Alzheimer's disease.

Katzman became convinced that Alzheimer's was far more widespread than most people thought. He believed that it had been widely misdiagnosed as normal-pressure hydrocephalus, senile dementia, and other dementing conditions. He studied figures on dementia among the elderly and estimated the percentage of those cases that were due to Alzheimer's disease. The results shocked him: Alzheimer's was the fourth or fifth most common cause of death in the United States.

In 1975, Katzman called on his fellow scientists to drop the term *senile dementia* altogether and include it under the diagnosis of Alzheimer's disease. In 1976, he wrote an editorial that detailed his findings about the death rate from Alzheimer's and asked his colleagues to take action against this silent killer. Katzman said,

> In focusing attention on the mortality [death] associated with Alzheimer's disease, our goal is not to find a way to prolong the life of severely demented persons, but rather to call attention to our belief that senile as well as presenile forms of Alzheimer are a single disease, a disease whose [cause] must be determined, whose course must be aborted, and ultimately a disease to be prevented.[10]

Katzman's work had a profound effect on the scientific community. As misdiagnoses were corrected and the true impact of Alzheimer's disease became apparent, the general public began to take notice. Beginning in the 1980s, television news shows, popular magazines, reputable newspapers, and supermarket tabloids were running stories on the horrors of Alzheimer's. Community service agencies developed day care programs for Alzheimer's patients and support groups for the family members who cared for them. Nursing homes set up special Alzheimer's wards for patients who needed institutional care.

Government agencies and private foundations funded numerous studies, seeking ways to prevent, cure, or at least delay the onset of Alzheimer's disease. From the beginning, there has been a sense of urgency in all this activity. The combination of a longer life span and a disease that robs those added years of meaning is a frightening one. If Alzheimer's disease is not conquered, millions will find their longevity to be a burden rather than a blessing.

Chapter 2

The Search for Answers

Since Alois Alzheimer's first case history, scientists have probed the mysteries of Alzheimer's disease. Some investigate the structural and chemical changes in the brain, while others concentrate on hereditary factors. Still others work to develop drugs and other treatments to combat the disease. All, however, share a common problem: The answers to Alzheimer's will be difficult to find because they lie within the brain, the most complex and least understood organ of the human body.

The brain processes millions of bits of information at a speed that puts the fastest computer to shame. This wrinkled, pinkish-gray mass of nerve tissue is the command center of the entire body.

Damage to a particular area of the brain also damages the function that area controls. For example, damage to the part of the brain that controls motor skills can cause uneven or jerky movements. Damage to the speech center can cause a partial or total loss of articulate speech. Alzheimer's strikes the centers of the brain that control memory and cognition, or thinking ability.

Alzheimer's and Memory

For many people, impaired memory is the most terrifying thing about Alzheimer's disease. Memory is critical to thinking and reasoning, and also to an individual's sense of personal identity. Thought does not happen in a vacuum. Everything from philosophical musings to decisions about what to have for dinner draws on a storehouse of collected facts and experiences.

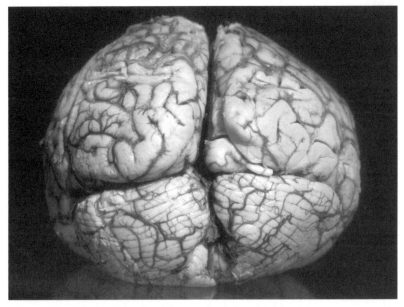

The human brain is the command center of the entire body.

The human memory is both personal and objective (related to factual knowledge). Factual memories define and describe the world. They enable a person to recall that two plus two is four, that fire is hot, that a touchdown in football is worth six points. Personal memories define individual identity and give meaning to life experiences.

Author and biologist Rebecca Rupp calls memory "the bedrock of our being." She says that memory allows us to "shape our characters, build our careers, forge our relationships, and . . . [create the] irreplaceable histories of ourselves. Without [memory], we are hollow persons, not only empty of a past, but lacking a foundation upon which to build the future."[11]

Types of Memory

Scientists have divided memory into three types, based on the length of time the memory is intended to last. Short-term, intermediate, and long-term memory not only perform different functions, they trigger different biochemical processes in the brain.

Short-term memory rearranges existing brain chemicals for a brief period. When the need for the memory passes, the cells return to their old arrangement. The information is forgotten. The common experience of looking up a phone number is a good example of short-term memory in action. The memory will last just long enough for the person to dial the phone.

This type of forgetting is not only normal but necessary. If a human being remembered every fact and experience, the information would eventually overwhelm the storage capacity of the brain. Remembering everything would also make reasoning more difficult. There would be so many scraps of memory that selecting, organizing, and evaluating them would become a hopeless task.

Intermediate-term memory stimulates the production of existing brain chemicals to create memories that will survive for hours instead of moments. The student who crams for a test is using intermediate memory. When the test is over, some of the information will be forgotten and some will be stored in long-term memory.

Long-term memory actually changes the structure of the brain. It creates new brain chemicals and new connections between cells. It contains personal and factual information along with procedural, or task-related, memories. According to Rebecca Rupp, procedural memory "is a process of knowing *how*. We know *how* to swim, *how* to dunk a basketball, *how* to play [the song] 'The Flight of the Bumblebee' on the violin. . . . Procedural memory is . . . what allows us, fifteen years after the fact, to hop back on a bicycle and . . . peddle away."[12]

The loss of procedural memory can be especially difficult for Alzheimer's patients and their caregivers. It interferes with daily life and makes patients increasingly helpless. Activities that were once automatic become challenging, and finally impossible. For example, people with normal brain functioning do not have to think about how to get dressed in the morning. People with moderate Alzheimer's disease have to think about each step in the process, what things to put on in what order. People in the severe stages of the disease no longer remember how to perform the process at all.

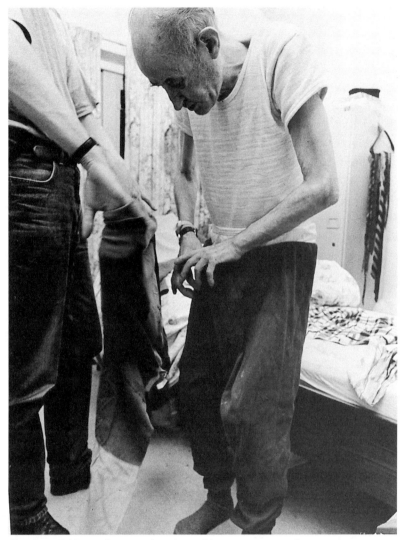

Simple activities such as getting dressed become more and more of a challenge for the Alzheimer's patient.

The Blighted Brain

Alzheimer's disease destroys memory by disrupting the delicate biochemistry of the brain. The human brain contains about 1 trillion neurons, or nerve cells. These cells are connected and regulated by different chemicals: neurotransmitters that carry nerve messages from cell to cell, and special proteins called enzymes that switch chemical processes on and off as needed.

Faulty brain chemistry is the likeliest cause of the plaques and tangles in the Alzheimer brain. The microscopic "freckles" known as plaques are composed of a substance known as beta-amyloid protein, or BAP. BAP is produced from a normal brain substance called amyloid precursor protein. Fragments of BAP clump together in a specific way to form insoluble deposits, or particles that cannot be dissolved.

The threadlike strands that bundle together to form tangles are composed mainly of a protein called tau. In its normal state, tau bonds with microtubules, structures in every cell that carry nutrients to all parts of a cell.

In Alzheimer's disease, tau is chemically altered, so it can no longer bond properly with the microtubules, which weaken and eventually collapse. Deprived of nutrients, the cell dies, leaving only tangles behind. Scientists have discovered that excessive amounts of the chemical phosphorus cause this breakdown in tau. They do not know, however, what triggers the abnormal buildup of phosphorus, or how it interacts with tau to cause the chemical changes.

The Importance of Plaques and Tangles

Despite the research into tau and amyloid proteins, the nature of plaques and tangles remains a mystery. Scientists know that both damage brain tissue, but they do not know how this damage occurs. They know that both play an important role in Alzheimer's disease, but the relationship between them is unclear.

Plaques and tangles may be equally important in producing Alzheimer's disease, or one may be secondary to the other. It is possible that one is the cause and the other a by-product of the disease. It is also possible that both are by-products of some as-yet-unidentified abnormality.

These uncertainties have provoked great debate in the scientific community. As Joseph Rogers explains,

> There has been considerable quibbling among Alzheimer's scientists over the relative importance of senile plaques and neurofibrillary tangles. Some . . . argue [that plaques are most

important]. . . . Others . . . argue just the opposite. . . . The fact is that plaques and tangles have been the defining hallmarks of Alzheimer's disease since Alois Alzheimer first noticed them in 1906. They are both associated with deterioration in the Alzheimer's brain, and they are both extremely important to unraveling the mysteries of Alzheimer's disease.[13]

The Third Hallmark

In 1997, this mystery became even more complex with the discovery of a third type of lesion, or abnormal growth, in Alzheimer's brains. It looks a great deal like an amyloid plaque but is made of

This computer graphic illustrates the difference in volume between a healthy section of the brain (left) and a section afflicted with Alzheimer's (right).

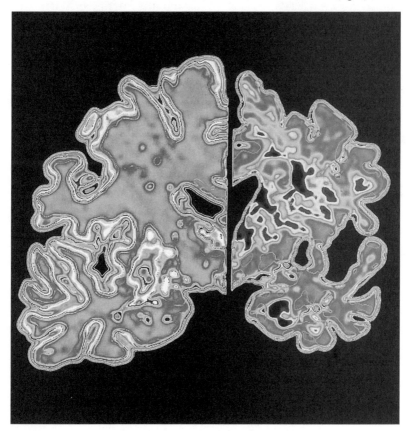

a previously unidentified protein. Doctors John Trojanowski and Virginia Lee of the University of Pennsylvania discovered it when they were studying the chemical properties of tangles.

The new protein, dubbed AMY117, escaped notice for some ninety years simply because of the way tissue specimens are prepared for viewing. The specimens are treated with chemical dyes that make abnormalities visible under the microscope. According to Virginia Lee, "The staining and chemical dye methods that have been used in the past to label Alzheimer's disease [abnormalities] . . . do not pick up this lesion. A new series of [stains] we created to explore elements of the neurofibrillary tangles [made the new lesion visible]."[14]

Scientists are hopeful that this discovery may one day produce significant advances in Alzheimer's research. "I feel very excited about it," neuroscientist Zaven Khachaturian told a writer for *Science* magazine. "This opens new vistas for us in terms of [understanding] what's happening in the disease, and it may even give us new diagnostic tools and new targets for treatment."[15]

The Acetylcholine Connection

More than twenty years before the discovery of AMY117, another substance was making news in Alzheimer's research. Scientists discovered that people with Alzheimer's had low levels of the neurotransmitter acetylcholine in their brains. The fact that acetylcholine is known to play an important role in memory opened an intriguing possibility: Perhaps Alzheimer's was an acetylcholine deficiency disease.

Deficiency diseases are well known to scientists. For example, diabetes is a deficiency disease caused by the lack of insulin, a hormone that processes sugar. Replacing this hormone enables the body to function more normally. If similar results could be achieved by replacing acetylcholine in Alzheimer's patients, an effective treatment might be close at hand. This prospect caused excitement throughout the scientific community.

However, scientists soon discovered problems with acetylcholine replacement therapy. Acetylcholine given by pills or injections was destroyed in the bloodstream before it ever reached the brain. So the scientists changed their tactics. Since they could not increase the brain's supply of acetylcholine, they began seeking ways to preserve what was already there. Because acetylcholine is broken down in the body by a chemical called acetylcholinesterase, researchers thought a drug that would inhibit (decrease or limit) the action of this chemical would slow down the loss of acetylcholine.

This line of research eventually led to the first anti-Alzheimer's drug, tacrine, which produced limited improvement in some patients with mild to moderate Alzheimer's disease. Unfortunately, it had no effect on people in advanced stages of the disease.

The Genetic Link

In the 1980s, Alzheimer's researchers began exploring the possibility that at least some forms of the disease were hereditary. Investigating this possibility took Alzheimer's research into the growing field of genetics.

Genetics is the branch of biology that deals with the mechanisms of heredity. The geneticist wants to know how organisms pass on their characteristics to other generations and how these characteristics affect the individual.

Genes are the basic units of heredity. They are arranged in a precise order on rodlike structures called chromosomes. An individual inherits twenty-three pairs of chromosomes, one set from each parent. They contain all the information necessary to create a human being.

When a mutation, or sudden change, in a gene alters the code, many disorders and diseases can result. Some genetic, or hereditary, disorders appear at birth. Others do not appear until later in life. It is also possible to carry a defective gene without developing symptoms at all. In such cases, the unaffected individual can still pass on the genetic flaw to his or her offspring, which, in turn, passes the defect to a new generation. The search for a familial, or family, form of Alzheimer's disease was prompted in part by genetic studies of two other diseases that devastate the brain: Huntington's chorea and Down's syndrome.

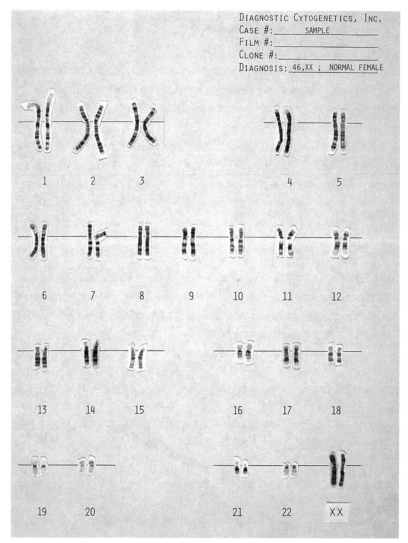

DIAGNOSTIC CYTOGENETICS, INC,
CASE #:_____SAMPLE_____
FILM #:_____
CLONE #:_____
DIAGNOSIS: 46,XX ; NORMAL FEMALE

Twenty-three pairs of chromosomes, as seen in this chart, contain all the information necessary to create a human being.

Genetics and Huntington's Disease

Huntington's chorea, also known as Huntington's disease, is a deadly neurological affliction. It first strikes the part of the brain that controls movement. According to the National Institute of Neurological Disorders and Stroke, "People affected with [Huntington's disease] writhe, twist, and turn in a constant, uncontrollable dance-like motion."[16]

The symptoms of Huntington's have been known since the Middle Ages. George Huntington, the physician who formally described the disease in 1872, was well aware that it had been around for a long time. He called the disorder "an heirloom from generations away back in the dim past."[17]

The hereditary nature of this "heirloom" has always been clear. The symptoms were easily recognizable, and obviously appeared in family groups. Until late in the twentieth century, however, the knowledge that Huntington's was hereditary had little practical value. When Huntington's was first described, the ability to isolate a particular gene and determine how it produced disease was decades away.

Not until the early 1980s did researchers find the genetic link to Huntington's disease. Dr. James Gusella and a team of researchers at Massachusetts General Hospital conclusively established that the defective gene was located on chromosome 4.

The impact of this discovery was felt throughout the scientific community. Gusella's team had accomplished something that had never been done before: pinpoint the abnormal gene responsible for a particular disease. In the process, they set a precedent, or example, for other researchers.

Scientists working on Alzheimer's disease soon picked up on that example. According to neurologist Daniel A. Pollen, the discovery of the Huntington's gene became the "decisive event that would in time trigger the systematic search for the genes causing [an inherited form] of Alzheimer's disease."[18]

Alzheimer's Disease and Down's Syndrome

Another discovery that influenced Alzheimer's research was a link with Down's syndrome. Down's is a genetic disorder that produces mild to moderate mental retardation. It is caused by a flaw on chromosome 21; instead of the normal two copies, people with Down's syndrome have three copies of chromosome 21.

It is not yet known what produces this extra copy, or exactly how it causes Down's syndrome. What researchers do know is that people with Down's syndrome are prone to develop Alzheimer's disease. According to Dr. Joseph Rogers, it has been "conclusively demonstrated that virtually all Down's syndrome patients over the age of 35 to 40 will show the brain changes of Alzheimer's disease."[19] Furthermore, a growing body of evidence connecting Alzheimer's and Down's raised the possibility that the link between the two diseases was genetic.

Biological Detectives

In 1984, biochemists George Glenner and Caine Wong discovered an important clue to that link. They learned that the amyloid protein found in the blood vessels of Down's brains was nearly identical to the amyloid found in Alzheimer's plaques. On the strength of these findings, Glenner and Wong suggested that "the presence of a common amyloid protein in both Down's syndrome . . . and Alzheimer's disease suggests the possibility that the genetic defect in Alzheimer's disease . . . is [located on] chromosome 21."[20]

Two years later, four research groups working independently of one another demonstrated that the gene that produces amy-

Researchers have found that people with Down's syndrome are more likely to develop Alzheimer's disease.

loid was indeed located on chromosome 21, as Glenner and Wong had suspected. Hope ran high that an answer to the puzzle of Alzheimer's was close at hand.

Less than a year later, however, new findings dashed that hope. Scientists discovered that only a small percentage of families with hereditary Alzheimer's had the amyloid defect on chromosome 21. This meant that something else must be at work. The ultimate answer to Alzheimer's disease was not as close as everyone had hoped.

Although this finding was disappointing, it did not mean that the research on chromosome 21 had been a failure. As Joseph Rogers said, "We now know exactly where the [amyloid] that makes up . . . plaques comes from, and we know that changes in the gene that codes for [amyloid] can cause Alzheimer's disease [in some cases]."[21]

Hannah's Gene

One of the most important ways of studying the genetics of Alzheimer's disease was to conduct careful studies of large family groups with a known history of the disease. The best known of these studies was "Hannah's family." This large family had a history of Alzheimer's that could be traced back to a woman named Hannah, who was born in Byelorussia or Latvia in 1844.

Little is known about Hannah's life. She and her husband Shlomo lived in a town called Ekatterinoslav and had nine children. The last child was born in 1888, when Hannah was forty-four years old. Only a few years later, Hannah developed the first symptoms of Alzheimer's disease.

Her exact age at the time of onset is unknown, but the children were not yet grown. A daughter born in 1883 told her own children about growing up in a household that functioned around the needs of her increasingly helpless mother.

Eventually, Alzheimer's disease struck four of Hannah's nine children and eleven of her thirty-four grandchildren. By the 1980s, a fourth generation was falling prey to the disease. The family came to scientific attention in May 1985, when one of Hannah's descendants arrived at the office of Dr. Daniel Pollen.

The fifty-one-year-old patient was well aware of his family's history of Alzheimer's disease. He brought a pedigree, or family tree, showing how the disease had progressed through Hannah's descendants.

Dr. Pollen quickly recognized the importance of this family tree. From one generation to the next, it showed every case of Alzheimer's disease, along with the age of onset. Such complete information would be invaluable to researchers. The same methods that uncovered the gene responsible for Huntington's disease might uncover the genetic origin of the Alzheimer's in Hannah's family.

For the next ten years, teams of researchers worked on the problem. They studied affected and unaffected members of Hannah's family, and compared those results with similar data from other family groups known to carry genetic Alzheimer's. On July 29, 1995, neurologist Peter St. George-Hyslop, who had worked on the chromosome 21 project, announced that his team had found Hannah's gene, a protein located on chromosome 14.

Drs. Peter St. George-Hyslop (left) and James Gusella scan a DNA pattern.

The discovery electrified the scientific world. As Daniel Pollen explained in his book *Hannah's Heirs,*

> With the discovery of Hannah's gene, the [obstacle] preventing further understanding of the [origins] of the majority of cases of early-onset Alzheimer's was now broken. The way was now open for scientists to discover how the new protein interacted with [amyloid and] . . . other proteins, to unravel the underlying sequence of events leading . . . to a devastating disease.[22]

The APOE Connection

The research into familial Alzheimer's began as an attempt to understand early-onset forms of the disease. Perhaps because of this focus, many scientists believed that early onset of symptoms was a defining characteristic of hereditary Alzheimer's disease. Late-onset forms were considered to be sporadic, or nonhereditary. In 1993, however, Dr. Allen Roses of Duke University made a discovery that raised doubts about this classification.

On chromosome 19, he found a gene that produces a substance called apolipoprotein E. The gene is called APOE for short; the substance it produces is called apoE. There are three distinct forms of apoE: E2, E3, and E4. Roses's study indicated that the E4 form might be a risk factor for late-onset Alzheimer's disease. People with E4 have a 29 percent chance of developing Alzheimer's; people without it have only a 9 percent chance of developing the disease.

The exact function of apoE is not clear, but scientists do know that it plays a role in the function of tau, the protein involved in the formation of Alzheimer's tangles. E4 does not combine properly with tau. This may be one of the reasons that tau malfunctions in Alzheimer's disease.

The discovery of APOE indicated that heredity may play a larger role in Alzheimer's than was previously thought. This possibility is only one of the issues confronting Alzheimer's research in the twenty-first century.

Amid all the unknowns and all the breakthroughs that turn into disappointments, one fact is clear: The problem of Alzheimer's

Dr. Allen Roses speaks during a November 1993 Alzheimer's disease conference in Washington, D.C.

disease will not be solved quickly or easily. A complete explanation would have to account for amyloid plaques, tau tangles, and the newly discovered abnormality called AMY117. It would have to account for genetic factors and for the acetylcholine deficiency in the memory center of the brain. Even when scientists can produce a profile that ties all these factors together and accounts for all cases, the work will not be over. The next step is to use that information as a foundation for research in the prevention and cure of Alzheimer's disease.

Chapter 3

Diagnosis

WHEN ALOIS ALZHEIMER first described the disease that bears his name, accurate diagnosis in a living subject was impossible. Only autopsy, or examination after death, could verify Alzheimer's disease.

Over the years, diagnostic methods improved. Doctors learned to evaluate risk factors and symptoms, and technology provided new equipment for sophisticated testing. By the end of the twentieth century, doctors could diagnose Alzheimer's disease with 90 percent accuracy. Certainty still requires an autopsy.

Acknowledging the Problem

In a sense, the diagnostic process starts when a patient or family member first recognizes that a problem exists. Often there is a considerable gap between the beginning of memory difficulties and the acknowledgment of the problem. The lapses and mistakes pile up until it becomes clear that they are not isolated incidents, but part of a pattern.

In many cases, one event will force the patient or a relative to notice that pattern. For Maureen Reagan, daughter of former president Ronald Reagan, that event was a conversation about one of her father's movie roles. She says,

> It was late in 1993 and we were having dinner with my father. We were discussing a 1950s film he made, "Prisoner of War." For years he had told me about the gruesome tortures inflicted on American prisoners by the North Koreans. But now he seemed to be hearing me tell the stories for the first time. Finally he looked at me and said, "Mermie, I have no recollection of making that movie."[23]

41

Maureen Reagan (left) said that when her father, former president Ronald Reagan, began having memory problems, the family realized something was wrong.

Less than a year later, Ronald Reagan was diagnosed with Alzheimer's disease. Not long afterward, newspapers reported that he had no memory of having been president of the United States.

Recognizing the Symptoms

The Reagan family's experience is not unusual. Spotting the problem can often be difficult because early symptoms of Alzheimer's can be attributed to stress, inattention, or simple absent-mindedness. If they are aware of the warning signs, however, family members, and even patients themselves, will be more likely to recognize that a problem exists. And a major part of that awareness is knowing

Being aware of the warning signs can help family members recognize early Alzheimer's in a loved one.

how the symptoms of early Alzheimer's differ from normal lapses in memory or mistakes in judgment.

The first of the five most common symptoms of Alzheimer's is that task-related difficulties are not limited to occasionally forgetting small details. For example, anyone could forget to put the salt in a favorite recipe. For Alzheimer's patients, though, the difficulties involve entire tasks. The person with Alzheimer's might be unable to put the recipe's ingredients together at all.

The second symptom, language problems, often begins with an inability to remember the proper names of things. Alzheimer's patients will sometimes fill in those gaps with inappropriate words or phrases, without being aware that they are doing so. They may produce sentences that are garbled and then become angry when others cannot understand what they are trying to say.

Probably one of the most frightening symptoms of early Alzheimer's is disorientation. Victims can lose their sense of time and place, the where and when of their own lives. They may believe they are living in a different time period or become hopelessly lost walking down a familiar street.

The fourth symptom, misplacing objects, can be a normal part of life. However, Alzheimer's patients lose things because they have placed them in wildly inappropriate places. For example, a person might put shoes in the refrigerator or store silverware in the washing machine.

Finally, as the person becomes increasingly unable to cope with life, he or she may become noticeably moody: cheerful one minute, furious or fearful the next. Longer-lasting changes can transform an even-tempered person into a bully, or a cheerful person into a chronic complainer.

These symptoms also appear in conditions other than Alzheimer's. However, when they appear together and grow worse over time, a doctor is likely to suspect Alzheimer's.

Understanding the Risks

In addition to considering symptoms, people who work with Alzheimer's disease take the patient's risk factors into account.

Diagnosis

Risk factors are traits or conditions that increase the likelihood that a person will develop any given disease. For example, a high level of cholesterol increases the risk of heart attack; smoking increases the risk of lung cancer. The chief risk factors for Alzheimer's disease are age, gender, and heredity.

Although old age increases everyone's risk of Alzheimer's disease, elderly women are more likely to be stricken than elderly men. The reason for this is not known. It could be an actual predisposition, some characteristic that females have and males do not. It could also be a product of statistics. Females live longer than males, so more of them may survive to develop Alzheimer's in extreme old age.

Unlike age and gender, genetic defects are not immediately apparent, so in preliminary screening, doctors rely on family history. According to Joseph Rogers, "If one or two of your first-order blood relatives (mother, father, sister, brother) has

Researchers have determined that age increases the risk of Alzheimer's disease.

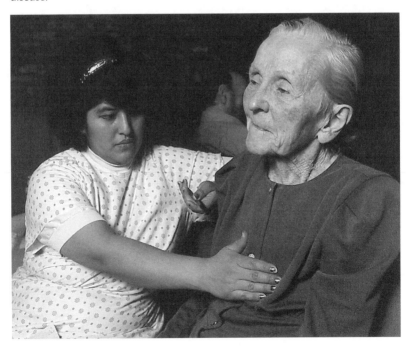

Alzheimer's . . . it increases the chances that you . . . will develop the disorder by as much as two to four fold."[24]

Because risk assessment deals in probabilities, not certainties, the fact that a person is in a high-risk category does not mean that he or she will develop Alzheimer's disease. It simply means that a doctor will take age, gender, and family history into account when deciding whether to proceed with the evaluation.

The Goals of Patient Evaluation

When a patient with symptoms of dementia first visits the doctor, it is the beginning of a lengthy process. The doctor must assess the patient's condition, identify or rule out other diseases that may be causing the dementia, and create a treatment plan that suits the patient's needs.

In their book *The 36-Hour Day*, Nancy L. Mace and Peter V. Rabins explain the seven things that a detailed patient evaluation should reveal:

1. the exact nature of the person's illness,

2. whether or not the condition can be reversed or treated,

3. the nature and extent of the disability,

4. the areas in which the person can still function successfully,

5. whether the person has other health problems that need treatment and that might be making [his or] her mental problems worse,

6. the social and psychological needs and resources of the sick person and the family or caregiver, and

7. the changes you can expect in the future.[25]

The First Steps in Diagnosis

To achieve these goals, the diagnostic process must be thorough. It begins with a complete physical examination and a detailed medical history. The physical assesses the patient's general health and detects problems that should be treated or studied further. The history is like a medical biography of the person. It

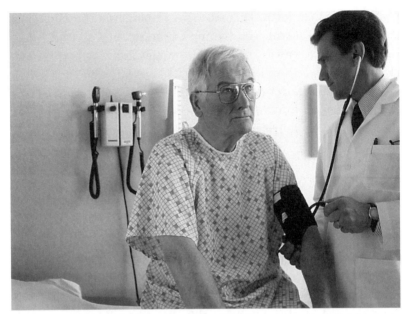

Diagnosing Alzheimer's disease can be a difficult process and cannot be determined through a physical examination alone.

covers everything from childhood illnesses to hospitalizations to chronic conditions such as diabetes or high blood pressure. The doctor also asks about the patient's family to determine if hereditary factors may be at work.

The medical history helps the doctor evaluate the patient as an individual rather than just a set of symptoms. By comparing the patient's medical history to his or her present condition, the doctor can note major changes in function or behavior.

Testing Mental Function

After the medical history and preliminary physical, the doctor often gives a mental function test. This is a standardized exam with questions that are carefully selected to assess different functions, such as memory, calculation, language, and spatial skills (the ability to deal with the relationship between objects).

People without brain impairment average twenty five to twenty-nine points out of a possible thirty on the Mini-Mental State Examination. A patient's first test shows how he or she compares to that norm. This score then becomes a "baseline." By repeating the test from time to time, that baseline gives the doctor an objective way of measuring changes in the patient's mental abilities.

In her book *Tangled Minds*, Dr. Muriel Gillick discusses the mental function tests of a patient she called Sylvia Truman. On the first test, Mrs. Truman showed good orientation; she knew the day, the date, the month, and the year. She could identify common objects such as glasses and a watch. Her skills of visualizing and dealing with spatial relationships, however, were more impaired. Gillick says,

> Drawing a clock face with all the numbers . . . [was] totally beyond her. She drew a circle that was far too small to accommodate the necessary numbers and then proceeded to put the numbers outside the circle, at first following the arc of her clock, but then abruptly proceeding horizontally.[26]

On that first exam, Sylvia Truman scored twenty out of a possible thirty. Three years later, she scored only fourteen out of thirty, indicating substantial decline in her mental abilities.

Looking for Other Explanations

The mental function test, physical exam, and medical history are the foundation of the evaluation process. The next step is to look for conditions besides Alzheimer's that may account for the patient's dementia. This process is called differential diagnosis.

Dr. Jeffrey Hull explains:

> A differential diagnosis is a working list of possibilities that a physician uses in the process of diagnosing a specific disease. . . . After listing mentally or on paper the possible conditions or diseases under consideration, the physician then compares what he knows about the case to the list of possibilities and begins to narrow the choices, discarding those that don't fit and [moving] the most likely candidates to the top of the list. It may then be necessary to perform additional [tests] to confirm or exclude the remaining possibilities.[27]

In dealing with Alzheimer's disease, the list will be long. Possible causes of dementia range from organ malfunction to vitamin or hormone deficiencies. Long-term alcohol or drug abuse can produce disorientation, memory loss, and personality changes. Strokes or tumors can damage the brain, thereby producing dementia.

When the doctor has produced a final list, he or she must then arrange to test for every possibility. The testing typically begins with several types of blood analysis. The doctor will also usually order a complete neurological (nervous system) exam to detect and rule out other conditions that produce dementia.

Blood Analysis

Blood analysis can reveal an amazing amount of information about diseases and conditions that can produce dementia that might be mistaken for Alzheimer's. Because many of these conditions are treatable or even curable, accounting for them is a crucial part of the diagnostic process.

Other tests reveal vitamin deficiencies and glandular disorders that may mimic Alzheimer's. For example, a simple blood test can identify low levels of folate, one of the B vitamins, which can produce memory problems and difficulties in coordination. Treatment with supplemental vitamins can eliminate these symptoms and restore the person to normal function.

A thyroid-stimulating hormone, or TSH, test

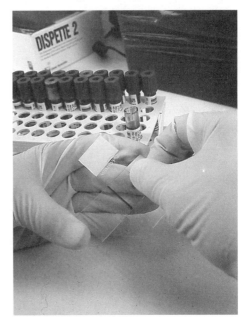

Blood analysis is a crucial step in diagnosing Alzheimer's disease.

checks the function of the thyroid gland. This small gland at the base of the throat produces a hormone that helps to regulate many body systems. Thyroid deficiencies can produce mental and emotional symptoms of dementia, such as forgetfulness and unexplained mood swings. Thyroid replacement therapy restores normal levels of the hormone and reverses the dementia.

Each normal result on the blood work eliminates another possible cause of the dementia. Abnormal, or even questionable, results will be followed up with more detailed examinations and tests.

Neurological Testing

The neurological workup, or detailed diagnostic study, is another important part of any evaluation for Alzheimer's disease. The doctor must screen for other diseases that damage the nervous system such as strokes, brain tumors, and non-Alzheimer's dementias. Any of these conditions may mimic some of the symptoms of Alzheimer's disease.

For example, the second leading cause of dementia is a condition known as multi-infarct dementia. This is a series of small strokes caused by the blockage of arteries in the brain. Each of these little strokes kills a small amount of brain tissue (the word *infarct* means "tissue death"). The damage accumulates over time, producing dementia.

A variety of tests are available to identify diseases of the brain and nervous system. These include lumbar punctures, electroencephalograms (EEGs), and several computer-assisted imaging technologies.

The lumbar puncture, or spinal tap, involves inserting a long needle into the small of the back and withdrawing fluid from around the spinal cord. Laboratory analysis of this fluid can detect evidence of tumors, inflammations, and infections, all of which can produce certain symptoms of dementia.

The EEG tests the electrical functions of the brain. Tiny sensors are placed on the head with a pastelike substance. The sensors send information to a machine that records brain-wave activity as zig-zag lines on a chart. A skilled neurologist then studies the pattern for evidence of tumors, head injuries, seizure disorders, and several other conditions.

A technician performs an EEG on a patient.

Finally, imaging tests, which are on the cutting edge of medical technology, use X rays, magnetic fields, or nuclear material to build complex, highly detailed views of a small section, or "slice," of a part of the body. Those tests are generally referred to by their initials, such as CT (X ray computed tomography), CAT (computer-assisted tomography), and MRI (magnetic resonance imaging).

Imaging technology is expensive and not readily available in some areas. Patients may have to travel to a university or large teaching hospital for their tests. For these and other reasons, many doctors do not order scans unless they have specific reasons for doing so. For example, if the patient has had a stroke or a severe injury to the head, the doctor may order an image text because he or she needs the precise information to identify the extent of the brain damage.

Psychiatric Evaluations

Some doctors also routinely order a psychiatric exam to screen for depression or other forms of mental illness that can mimic Alzheimer's or make it worse. Others will order the psychiatric evaluation only if they have reason to suspect that mental illness is causing or complicating the patient's dementia. For example, anxiety disorders or depression can cause difficulties with memory, changes in personality, and lapses in judgment. Other disorders produce bizarre behavior, mood swings, or difficulty with language, all of which can appear to be symptoms of Alzheimer's.

Even when the diagnosis of Alzheimer's disease is fairly certain, a psychiatric evaluation can benefit many patients. Although there is no evidence that mental illness accelerates the brain damage of Alzheimer's, it can make symptoms worse. For example, depression is fairly common in patients who have Alzheimer's disease. This is particularly true during the early stages, when patients retain enough function to know that something is wrong with them. They may understand that the disease is incurable and will get worse over time.

Under such circumstances, it is hardly surprising that many patients become depressed. Treatment with antidepressant medications, though, can improve the patient's functioning and quality of life.

Diagnosis and Prognosis: The Moment of Truth

After the doctor has ruled out all the alternatives, a diagnosis of Alzheimer's disease is justified. When patients and their families hear the news, they may react in a number of different ways: hor-

Although patients and their loved ones all react differently to the diagnosis of Alzheimer's, most generally have the same question: What happens now?

ror, grief, or perhaps resignation. Whatever the reaction, diagnosis answers some questions but raises others.

Most of these questions will be variations of a single theme: What happens now? Generally, the doctor's first response is to give his or her prognosis, or a prediction of the probable course and outcome of the disease. Because the prognosis for Alzheimer's disease is grim, many doctors find this the most difficult part of the evaluation process.

Some of these physicians become deliberately vague. They speak of memory problems instead of dementia. They don't mention the name Alzheimer's disease or deal with the fact that it is progressive and eventually fatal. Others, however, become detached, impersonal, and brutally frank. Most fall somewhere in between.

According to Dr. Muriel Gillick,

What counts at least as much as *whether* to tell is *how* to tell. How the physician reveals the diagnosis must vary depending on the patient's ability to understand. Just as a patient with cancer does not necessarily need to be told the [progression of symptoms], the life expectancy, all possible treatments and each of their likely outcomes on the first office visit, so, too, the patient with dementia does not have to be hit over the head with the whole truth and nothing but the truth.[28]

However the doctor gives the news, both the patient and his or her family are likely to need help dealing with it. Unfortunately, there is nothing the doctor or anyone else can say that provides much comfort. After all the talking is done, the patient and his or her family are left to deal with what they can only see as a tragedy in the making.

Chapter 4

Treatment

WHEN A DISEASE is incurable, relentlessly progressive, and always fatal, treatment is necessarily restricted. In the case of Alzheimer's, doctors use existing therapies to control symptoms as much as possible. They also give routine medical care and treat illnesses or injuries as they arise. Psychotherapists and social workers deal with the emotional and social consequences of the disease. Caregivers cope with daily routines and try to help the patient stay involved in day-to-day life for as long as possible.

The Alzheimer's Drugs

At the end of the twentieth century, only two drugs specifically targeting a presumed cause of Alzheimer's disease were on the market in the United States. Tacrine, brand name Cognex, was approved by the Food and Drug Administration (FDA) in 1993. Donepezil, or Aricept, followed in 1996. Both drugs work by inhibiting the enzyme that destroys acetylcholine in the brain.

For some people in the early or middle stages of Alzheimer's, these drugs improve mental function. The improvement, however, is temporary. According to Dr. Ronald C. Petersen, director of the Mayo Clinic Alzheimer's Disease Center, "Neither tacrine nor donepezil can stop or reverse the disease. In addition, it remains unclear how long patients should take them or even how long the drugs will be effective."[29]

In some cases, the benefits can be of extremely short duration. In an article for *Newsweek* magazine, journalist Geoffrey Cowley told of one such case:

> William Van Zandt [an Alzheimer's patient] . . . started taking Aricept in 1997. "Within a week, there was such a noticeable

difference," his son Billy recalls. "He went from being completely uncommunicative to forming whole sentences." But Van Zandt resumed his decline eight weeks later, and after six months the family dropped the drug.[30]

Doctors and caregivers do their best to treat the symptoms of the Alzheimer's patient by using a combination of drugs and by maintaining daily routines and activities.

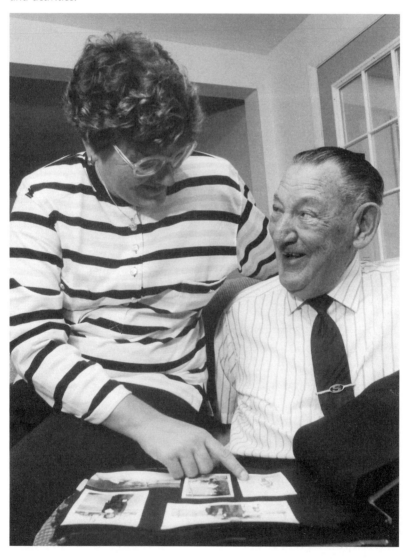

For most patients, the benefits of Aricept last longer than they did for William Van Zandt. But sooner or later, the drug always becomes ineffective. In addition to this, there are side effects, or unintended results. One side effect of Aricept, for example, is nausea, especially at the beginning of treatment.

Tacrine has an even more serious side effect: In 30 percent of patients studied, it interfered with liver function. Patients placed on tacrine must be monitored with regular blood tests to check liver function. If they develop liver problems, treatment must be discontinued immediately. For this reason, tacrine had fallen into disuse by the end of the twentieth century.

Though tacrine and donepezil have produced only modest results, Alzheimer's researchers are not yet ready to give up on drugs that preserve acetylcholine levels in the brain. By 1998, ten different drugs were in various stages of testing by the FDA.

In September 1999, a drug called galantamine, brand name Reminyl, was submitted to the FDA. Like other drugs in this class, galantamine curbs the enzyme that destroys acetylcholine in the brain. Unlike these other drugs, however, galantamine acts on nicotine receptors. Nicotine, the familiar villain of cigarette smoke, seems to stimulate the release of acetylcholine, although doctors do not recommend smoking as a part of treatment. Instead, it is a nicotine-like substance in galantamine that provides the benefit.

Drugs for Psychological Symptoms

Psychotropics, drugs that affect perception and mood, may also be useful in managing the symptoms of Alzheimer's disease. Patients who are agitated or depressed can sometimes benefit from antianxiety or antidepressant drugs. Those who see or hear things that aren't there, or believe that somebody is plotting against them, may be helped by drugs developed to treat psychosis, a loss of contact with reality.

When a patient with dementia develops psychotic symptoms, the result is a sharp and sudden decline in functioning. Treatment with antipsychotic medications, however, can sometimes restore the patient's mental function to its former level. For example, one

Alzheimer's patients suffering from agitation, depression, or loss of contact with reality can be treated with drugs to ease their symptoms.

of Dr. Muriel Gillick's patients who had developed psychotic symptoms became convinced that she was being held prisoner by a hired caregiver. In *Tangled Minds,* Dr. Gillick quotes the patient's jumbled accusations: "That woman's a guard. You should never have let her near the children. What do you know about her past? What did she do during the war? Did you check her record? . . . You can't be too careful."[31]

This outburst was only part of a pattern of paranoia, or extreme suspiciousness and fear. Dr. Gillick prescribed a low dose of the antipsychotic drug Haldol, and after a few days the patient's paranoia lessened.

Promising Treatments and Preventatives

In addition to treatment with acetylcholine replacements and psychotropic drugs, scientists began to identify other substances that might be useful in preventing or treating Alzheimer's disease. These include anti-inflammatory drugs used for the treatment of arthritis, the female hormone estrogen, and vitamin E.

The group of medicines classified as nonasteroidal anti-inflammatory drugs, or NSAIDs, came to the attention of Alzheimer's researchers in the 1980s. Inflammations are caused by irritation, injury, or infection in a specific area of the body. An inflammation may be red, swollen, and painful. Arthritis is a common disease produced by the inflammation of joints such as elbows or knees.

Investigators noticed that people taking drugs such as Advil and Motrin for arthritis showed a significantly lower rate of Alzheimer's than the general population. Several other studies produced evidence that supported this finding. One study tracked patients' use of NSAIDs over a long period of time. According to an article in *American Family Physician* magazine, the results indicated that "the risk of developing Alzheimer's disease was . . . about 50 percent less in those who were using NSAIDs."[32]

Like NSAIDs, estrogen has produced a great deal of excitement among Alzheimer's researchers. In 1997, the National Institute on Aging, or NIA, released the results of a study that tracked 472 women for a period of sixteen years. It showed

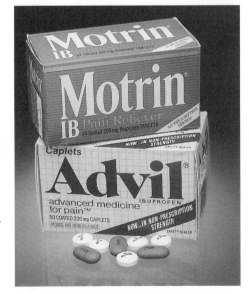

Some studies suggest that anti-inflammatory drugs may aid in the prevention of Alzheimer's.

that "estrogen replacement therapy in [older] women was associated with a 50 percent reduction in the risk of developing Alzheimer's disease."[33]

A study concluded in February 2000, however, failed to find similar benefits in women who already had the disease. After studying 120 women with mild to moderate Alzheimer's, the researchers announced that "taking estrogen did not lead to an improvement in mental skills or in the ability to carry out daily activities."[34]

These results do not necessarily conflict with each other. It is possible that estrogen is a preventative but not a treatment. Scientists hope that further studies will clarify the problem. In the meantime, the Mayo Clinic recommends that "estrogen [should not be] prescribed solely for its protective effects against memory loss and Alzheimer's. But it may offer that added benefit to women already taking it for other reasons."[35]

Vitamin E faired better in trials with patients who had moderate Alzheimer's disease. Vitamin E is an antioxidant, meaning that it helps remove toxic wastes from the body. It has been tested alone and in combination with the drug selegeline, a related substance that also has an antioxidant effect. The results have been promising. According to Dr. Vincent Delagarza,

> A study published in the April 24, 1997, issue of the *New England Journal of Medicine* reported that people with moderate Alzheimer's disease who were given . . . selegeline or high doses of vitamin E experienced a slowing of the progression of the disease by 7 months. Specifically, selegeline, vitamin E or a combination of the two delayed death, loss of the ability to do daily activities, moves into nursing homes, and progression to severe dementia.[36]

In October 1999 a new type of drug was added to the growing list of substances that may protect against Alzheimer's disease. A major study of fifty thousand patients found that the anticholesterol drugs lovastatin and pravastatin reduced the risk of Alzheimer's disease by 60 to 73 percent. Although further studies are needed to confirm these results, researchers regard the protective effect of these drugs as promising.

General Health Care for Alzheimer's Victims

When caring for an Alzheimer's victim, treatment includes more than controlling symptoms. The patient's general health must be carefully monitored as well. As Mace and Rabins explain,

> People with dementing illnesses can also suffer from other diseases ranging from relatively minor problems, like the flu, to serious illnesses. They may not be able to tell you they are in pain (even if they are able to speak well) or they may neglect their bodies. Cuts, bruises, or even broken bones can go unnoticed. People who sit or lie for long periods of time may develop pressure sores. Their physical health may gradually decline. *Corrections of even minor physical problems can greatly help people who suffer from dementing illness.*[37]

Patients with Alzheimer's may not be able to communicate their health problem, so doctors and caregivers must monitor them carefully.

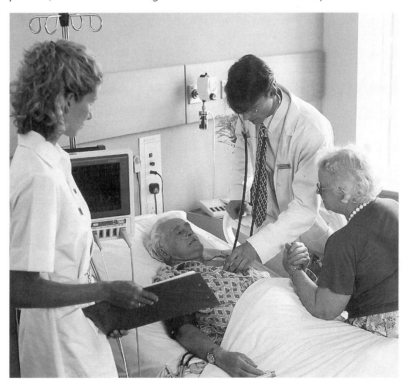

Some of these physical problems arise from the normal process of aging. For example, difficulties with vision and hearing are common in old age. When they occur in Alzheimer's patients, however, these problems can make the dementia appear worse than it is.

Not all relationships between dementia and physical problems are so clear-cut. Illness or injury can interact with dementia in unusual ways. For example, shortly before Elizabeth P. was diagnosed with Alzheimer's disease, she fell and broke her wrist. When the cast prevented her from doing many routine chores, her neighbors pitched in to help. A friend wrote out checks for Elizabeth's monthly bills and balanced the bank statement. Others helped with meal preparation, laundry, and house cleaning. One man even took Elizabeth's dog for its morning walks.

To the surprise of everyone who knew her, Elizabeth was not anxious for the cast to come off. When it did, she insisted on wearing an elastic wrist brace. The wrist still ached, she said, and her hand was weak and uncoordinated. The doctor couldn't understand what was wrong.

In time, Elizabeth's problem became clear. She needed the help she was getting because she could no longer remember how to write a check, prepare a meal, or do many other routine tasks. The injury allowed her to get help without having to admit that her mental function was slipping.

Nonmedical Therapies

In addition to medical treatment, a variety of psychological therapies help Alzheimer's victims experience satisfaction in their lives despite their deficiencies. The treatments are not cures, but they encourage patients to function as well as they can. By participating in these nonmedical or psychological therapies, for instance, someone who can't relate to the present may still be able to recall fragments of the past. Someone who can no longer carry on a conversation may be able to sing a song or enjoy a dance.

Most Alzheimer's care facilities offer several types of psychological therapy. Some of the more common methods are reminiscence and life review, remotivation, reality orientation, and validation. Each has its own particular strengths, and the challenge caregivers face is matching those strengths with the needs of individual patients. Many factors must be taken into account. For example, patients who are severely disruptive or violent cannot be put into group settings. Those who are unable to talk cannot participate in programs that require verbal skill.

In addition, therapists must set realistic goals. This means accepting the fact that nobody will be cured or even dramatically improved. Patients will forget much of what they have learned or experienced from one meeting to the next.

Perhaps the most important benefit of therapy is simply that it provides meaningful activity. Keeping Alzheimer's patients as mentally and physically active as possible can help to reduce problem behaviors. In part, this is because activity reduces boredom.

Engaging in activities is important for Alzheimer's patients as it helps reduce problem behaviors and boredom.

As Mace and Rabins point out in *The 36-Hour Day*, many Alzheimer's patients "have nothing to do but sit with vacant time and empty thoughts. . . . Restlessness, wandering, trying to go 'home,' repetitive motions, asking the same questions over and over . . . and many other behaviors begin as an effort to fill this emptiness."[38]

Reminiscence Therapy

Reminiscence therapy is one nonmedical treatment that attempts to fill the emptiness with the patient's own memories. It takes advantage of the fact that elderly people remember the remote past much better than they remember recent events. In studies of memory at various life stages, psychologist David Rubin found that older people "produce a large proportion of memories from the second and third (and occasionally first) decades of life. This mass of early-life memories generates a . . . hump toward the bottom of the forgetting curve."[39]

At its simplest level, this means that older memories are more durable than newer ones. According to biologist Rebecca Rupp, this is because of "the very nature of the memories themselves. During our teens and twenties . . . we are experiencing the bulk of our life's 'first-times': first leap off the high diving board, first day of college, first apartment, first meeting with your future parents-in-law. All these firsts . . . are great grist for memory's mill."[40]

Reminiscence therapy allows Alzheimer's patients to recapture these memories before the disease wipes them out forever. A typical group meeting is guided by a leader who starts by bringing up a topic of interest to one or more of the group members. Journalist Kate O'Rourke described a typical reminiscence program:

> Every day at Sunrise Assisted Living [Center] . . . some 10 people get together and chat about the good old days when Duke Ellington, Guy Lombardo and Benny Goodman [big band musicians] were kings and doctors made house calls.

> And with music from the big band era playing in the background, it would be easy to assume that this is merely a social gathering. It's not.

This is Sunrise's daily "reminiscing hour," a main component in its reminiscence therapy program whose goal is to stimulate the memory of residents in its Alzheimer's unit.[41]

According to psychiatrist Constantine Lyketsos, reminiscence therapy sessions such as these can produce immediate benefits: "The results might be that the person is calmer, a little bit better oriented, or perhaps sleep better for a short time after the treatment."[42] In the world of Alzheimer's treatment, even these modest results are welcome.

Remotivation

Like reminiscence therapy, remotivation stimulates mental activity. However, it does not focus on personal memories, problems, or feelings. Instead, each group session revolves around a common and noncontroversial topic like pets, holidays, hobbies, or vacations. The aim is to resocialize patients and reorient them to the real world.

In a sense, remotivation is an exercise in social conversation, or small talk. Groups meet once or twice a week, under the leadership of a nursing assistant or volunteer. The leader keeps the conversation on track and encourages everyone to participate in the discussion.

Objectivity is one of the keys to successful remotivation sessions. Leaders focus discussions on outer reality rather than on inward feelings. Remotivation therapist Jason Meixsell uses the example of a rainbow to illustrate the focus of discussions: "The objective aspects of a rainbow would include that it appears in the sky when the sun shines and it is raining. The colors of the rainbow would also be objective. These aspects of a rainbow are objective because they are all things that all people see when they look at a rainbow."[43] Subjective aspects (observations that vary from person to person) like how the patients feel when they see a rainbow would not be part of the discussion.

Another key to successful remotivation therapy is concentration on functional areas of the patient's personality. According to Meixsell, "remotivation does not attempt to work with the aspects of a person which have been effected by a mental or physical illness.

Remotivation works with the healthy or unwounded areas and works to enhance these areas."[44]

For Alzheimer's patients who still possess verbal skills, this type of therapy can be helpful. It offers a nonthreatening way to interact with others and focus on objective reality. Ideally, each patient leaves the remotivation session with the feeling that he or she made worthwhile contributions to the conversation. This in itself is a boost to the person's self-esteem.

Reality Orientation

Another technique that is intended to keep patients in contact with their world is reality orientation. In some Alzheimer's care facilities, the effort goes on round the clock and involves every staff member. For example, the nursing assistant who wakes patients might greet them with a pleasant "good morning," and then give them concrete information (like the time and the date) to start their day. Variations on this information will be repeated at every opportunity, throughout the day.

In addition to these routine announcements, staff members correct people whose statements or responses to questions do not reflect reality. For example, according to Naomi Feil, "A 90-year-old woman who remarks that she needs to visit her mother might be told 'You are 90 years old. Your mother is no longer alive.'"[45]

Some care facilities reinforce this ongoing process with daily classes. These may be led by a nursing assistant or an orderly. The leader uses visual aids such as clocks, calendars, menus, and bulletin boards to help patients keep a grip on reality.

This approach works best with mildly impaired people who are still trying to hold on to the real world. More severely impaired people, however, may withdraw or become angry when confronted with reality. Some are no longer capable of functioning in present time. Others could do so with effort, but they prefer a familiar and comforting past to a present that is filled with debility and loss.

Validation

Validation therapy, on the other hand, neither attempts to orient patients to the present nor helps them understand the past. In-

Maintaining a routine and participating in meaningful activities such as watering plants helps keep Alzheimer's patients oriented to the real world.

stead, validation therapists simply accept their patients' sense of time. They do not challenge errors in judgment or memory. Their goal is to improve the patient's life by validating, or accepting, him or her—faded memories, irrational fears, and all.

In group settings, validation therapists use a variety of activities to accomplish this goal. According to social worker Naomi Feil, the creator of validation therapy, "Music, movement, talk, and sharing food are the ingredients of a Validation group."[46]

The conversation in validation groups has a different focus than that in reminiscence or remotivation therapies. Instead of reminiscing about the past or making factual observations about the real world, patients in validation groups talk about feelings. According to Feil, "Topics should relate to emotions and unmet human needs such as love, belonging, the search for meaning and identity, the need to be active and useful, and the need to express emotions and be heard by a trusted other."[47] Discussion subjects include such questions as "How does one find meaning in life?" and "What happens when a person gets old?"

This is very different from the objective approach of remotivation therapy. Feil believes that confronting emotional issues can be satisfying for people who are still able to do so. It allows them to acknowledge their feelings in a supportive environment. This simple act of self-expression can make many people feel better.

Not all group members will be able to participate in conversation, but even nonverbal participants can enjoy music and movement activities. For example, dancing is often satisfying even for

The rhythm and movement of dancing can be satisfying and soothing for even the most severely impaired patients.

severely impaired patients. Alzheimer's disease affects the thinking centers of the brain, not the movement centers. Therefore, a person who can no longer talk or recognize familiar faces may be able to enjoy rhythmic movement. He or she may also be able to sing old, familiar songs. Feil says,

> When words have gone, familiar, early learned melodies return. . . . People . . . who no longer retain the ability to speak can often sing a lullaby from beginning to end. When a former sailor, now 95 years old . . . paces back and forth, his daughter [sings the Navy song] "Anchors Away, My Boys." The sailor stops, looks at his daughter, smiles, and sings with her. The sailor does not recognize his 60-year-old-daughter, nor does he know the name of the song, but he sings each word. His daughter can now communicate with music. She sings with her father since he can no longer talk.[48]

In validation, simple communication is the goal. The validator does not try to change the patient, teach new ways of coping, or correct mistaken ideas. He or she does not respond to the patient's behavior but to the emotions behind that behavior. This means that the validator does not challenge what the patient believes to be true, even when that belief appears to be absurd.

Differences In Therapies

Such an approach is the exact opposite of the focus in reality orientation. It is a difference that produces a very different exchange. For example, Naomi Feil describes how someone using reality orientation might handle an interchange with a disoriented patient:

> Mrs. K.: "Doctor, I have to go home now to feed my children."

> Physician: "Mrs. K, you can't go home. Your children are not there. You are 96 years old. Your children are grown and live far away."

> Mrs. K.: "Oh, Doctor I know all that. That's why I have to get out of here, right now. I have to feed them. They're coming home for lunch, and the door is locked. Get me out of here!"[49]

This same encounter would be very different with validation therapy:

Mrs. K.: "Doctor, I have to go home now to feed my children."

Physician: "What will you feed them?"

Mrs. K.: "Oh, Doctor, I am a good mother." (The patient here confuses present and past time.) "They love tuna. Do you think that's good for them?"

Physician: "It has a lot of protein. Is that what you fed your children? Do your grandchildren eat tuna?"

Mrs. K.: "They love it. I brought them all up right!" (The patient now moves between past fantasy and present reality. When her need to be a good mother is expressed, she can place herself in present time.)[50]

Sooner or later, Mrs. K will not be able to talk about tuna sandwiches at all. That is the way it is with Alzheimer's disease; gains are always temporary. That does not mean they are any less real or important, however. Even short-term gains improve the quality of patients' lives. Until Alzheimer's can be prevented or cured, this is the goal of every drug and nonmedical therapy.

Chapter 5

The Human Equation

IN THE RESEARCH laboratory, Alzheimer's disease is a scientific problem. In the home, the hospital, or Alzheimer's care facilities, it is a human problem. The challenges begin when the patient is diagnosed and do not end until he or she dies.

Newly diagnosed patients and their families face some hard choices. They must develop a care plan, make legal and financial arrangements, and deal with the fact that their lives have changed forever.

A doctor consults with a newly diagnosed Alzheimer's patient and her family.

Making Living Arrangements

For people newly diagnosed with Alzheimer's disease, living arrangements are often the most immediate concern. Deciding where to live is complicated by the fact that Alzheimer's is a progressive disease. What will work in the early stages will not work in the later ones.

This is because of the relentless progression of Alzheimer's disease. In the early stages, patients have trouble remembering recent events. Their general knowledge and memory of the past, however, may be relatively intact. They become easily confused and take longer with routine chores, but with help most can function adequately.

The picture is very different in the later stages. Patients may see or hear things that aren't there. They can no longer function independently, even for brief periods. In the final stages, they lose the ability to communicate and to recognize other people. They often become bedridden, completely dependent on others for the ordinary routines of daily care. It is simply a reality that care planning in the early stages should provide for necessary changes in the later ones.

When Alzheimer's symptoms are mild, many people remain in their own homes. When this becomes impossible, though, the person may move in with an adult child or other relative. The next step may be an assisted living facility, where the person receives help with daily routines but otherwise remains fairly independent. When symptoms become severe, round-the-clock care in a nursing home or specialized Alzheimer's facility may be the best option.

In many cases, patients who participate in planning where they will live as the disease progresses resist moving when the time actually arrives. Change is threatening to people who are losing their ability to deal with the world. Moving means having to cope with new situations at a time when their ability to do that is severely diminished. Unfortunately, there is no way to prevent this reaction. It happens even in the best-planned arrangements.

For example, Alzheimer's patient Elizabeth P. and her daughter sat down together and decided that Elizabeth would eventually go to a specialized Alzheimer's care facility near her daughter's home. In order to assure herself a place when the time came, Elizabeth put her name on the waiting list. By the time a place opened up, however, she could no longer remember the plans she had made. While her daughter and son-in-law packed her possessions, Elizabeth wandered after them, crying. She screamed when they tried to put her in the car, and begged neighbors to call the police, saying she was being kidnapped.

The situation of Elizabeth P. and her family is an excellent example of why advanced planning is so important: "I felt awful . . . like a traitor, an ungrateful child," said Elizabeth's daughter. "I don't think I could have gone through with it if mother herself hadn't made the plans when she was able."[51]

Dealing with Financial and Legal Issues

In addition to planning where the patient will live as the illness progresses, the family must arrange for someone to handle the patient's affairs when he or she is no longer able to do so, and to plan how to pay for long-term care. Alzheimer's disease is not only debilitating, it is costly. According to the Alzheimer's Association, the average cost of lifetime care for a patient with dementia is $174,000. Nursing homes average $42,000 a year.

Because of the cost, private health insurance does not cover this type of long-term care. Public sources of funding are also limited. And Medicaid, a government program for people with limited financial resources, helps pay for long-term care only after the patient has used all his or her own assets.

In the 1990s, many insurance companies began to offer special long-term care policies that pay about $100 per day for up to three years of care. According to "Kipplinger's Retirement Report," cost ranges from about $1,170 per year for a sixty-year-old to $4,100 for a seventy-five-year-old. A few companies will insure people up to the age of eighty-five, with substantially higher premiums.

In addition to deciding where the patient will live and how to pay for the care, Alzheimer's patients and their families face a number of other issues. If the patient is not able to deal with

Decisions on how to care for a family member with Alzheimer's are complicated by the fact that the disease is progressive.

these issues, next of kin or a court-appointed representative will step into the breach. If the patient is still able to make decisions, he or she might make a will and execute a power of attorney. A will is a legal document in which the person states how his or her assets are to be distributed after death. A power of attorney names another person, usually a spouse or adult child, to manage affairs when the patient is no longer able to do so.

The Challenge of Home Care

Caring for the daily needs of an Alzheimer's patient is both demanding and stressful for the caregiver. Many people have to quit good jobs, give up friends and social activities, and build their lives around the needs of an increasingly helpless patient.

For example, after Norman Pelham was stricken with Alzheimer's, his wife, Joan, gave up her job to take care of him. In an article for *Macleans* magazine, journalist Susan McClelland explained the challenge of this "grueling and emotionally draining 24-hour responsibility unique to Alzheimer's." McClelland writes that Joan Pelham "had to keep her husband from harming himself or from wandering away from their home. . . . Some nights, Norman would awaken, and . . . move iron bed frames, mattresses, cupboards and bookshelves—for no reason. Sometimes he had nightmares, and on two occasions, he attacked his wife while she slept. In the mornings, he never remembered a thing."[52]

Many communities have public and private resources to help family caregivers. Home health agencies can supply professional nurses or health aides to help regularly or on an as-needed basis. Adult day care programs also give family members a break from their routine and provide social interaction for patients.

A typical adult day care program costs around $39 a day. In some communities, at least part of this care is free to the patient and his or her family. For example, the Del Oro Caregiver Resource Center in Sacramento, California, provides vouchers to

Caring for a loved one with Alzheimer's at home is demanding, stressful, and emotionally draining for the caregiver.

pay for sixteen hours of respite care each month. Some caregivers use those sixteen hours for much-needed breaks in their daily routine. Others use them as part of an often-complicated plan to provide for a loved one during working hours.

Jim Burns is an example of someone in the second group. He works full-time while caring for his wife, Ruth. His voucher helps pay for three days per week at the adult day care center. For the rest of the work week, Burns pays $100 per day for Ruth to stay in a private home.

Learning How to Be a Caregiver

Dealing with the day-to-day consequences of Alzheimer's is not something that comes naturally to most people. Caregivers have to learn how to protect the patient, simplify his or her daily routines, and keep behavior problems at a minimum.

The first concern of most family caregivers is making the home safe for the patient. Anything that could be hazardous if misused must be locked away. For example, medicines, household cleaners, and certain toiletries can be dangerous to an Alzheimer's patient. So can power tools and ordinary electrical appliances. A water heater set too high can result in painful scalds if the patient forgets to adjust the temperature at the faucet.

In addition to making the environment safe for the patient, caregivers must try to make it as simple and predictable as possible. Perhaps because their mental world is so disorderly, Alzheimer's patients like structure and routine. Their daily schedules should be almost rigid—everything at a certain time and in a certain order. For example, if the person always gets up at 7:00, bathes, dresses, and eats breakfast, the mornings will go more smoothly.

Variations in this routine can stress the patient and cause behavior problems. When changes must be made, caregivers handle the situation in different ways. Some try to explain to the person. Others just go about the new routine very matter-of-factly. Whatever they decide, people who work with Alzheimer's patients stress the fact that there is no right or wrong way to handle these situations. The right way is whatever works best with a particular individual.

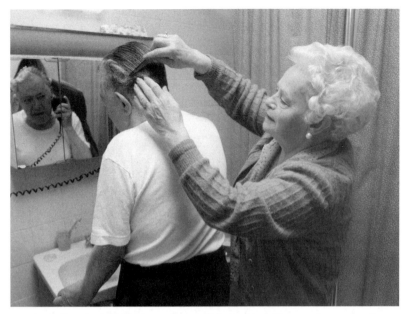

A strict daily schedule for the at-home Alzheimer's patient and caregiver is a must to help prevent stress, and behavior problems in the patient.

The Emotional Realities of Caregiving

Regardless of how many coping strategies caregivers use, the job of caring for an Alzheimer's victim is enormous. Caregivers must deal with anger, grief, and crushing fatigue. Often, it is a vicious circle: Fatigue and depression provoke anger, which in turn provokes guilt; guilt then makes the depression worse.

Guilt lies especially heavy on caregivers who had troubled relationships with the sick person. Authors Mace and Rabins give the example of one caregiver whose guilt about the past made it difficult for her to make decisions in the present. They write,

> Mrs. Dempsey had never liked her mother. As soon as she could she had moved away from home and called her mother only on special occasions. When her mother developed a dementing illness, [Mrs. Dempsey] brought her mother to live with her. The confused woman disrupted the family, kept everyone up at night, upset the children, and left Mrs.

Dempsey exhausted. When the doctor recommended that her mother enter a nursing home, Mrs. Dempsey only became more upset. She could not bring herself to put her mother in a nursing home even though this clearly would be better for everyone.[53]

Long-ago promises can also interfere with judgment. For example, at the age of sixteen, Sunday Isom promised her mother that she would never put her into a nursing home. When Isom was in her midthirties, her mother, Georgianna, was diagnosed with Alzheimer's disease. After Isom began caring for her mother at home, she realized the consequences of her youthful promise:

> When I look at my mother, who took care of me when I was a child, and she is reduced to being even less than a child, it is hard to see this on a day-to-day basis. I have to remember that this is a disease. Sometimes, I feel that if I shake her or slap her, it will go away. But I know that's not going to work, either.[54]

One potential problem of caring for an Alzheimer's patient at home is the strain on the relationship between patient and caregiver.

To deal with these feelings, doctors and other professionals recommend that caregivers join support groups. According to Alzheimers.com, an Internet source on Alzheimer's disease, support groups allow "people facing similar challenges [to] come together with dignity, compassion, and cooperation to share their experiences, gain perspective, offer and receive advice, and feel the profound comfort [of] being around others who know exactly what they're going through."[55]

Support groups help caregivers take even the most bizarre behaviors in stride. Just knowing that other people have trouble coping with certain behaviors can be reassuring, and as a result, the caregiver will be less likely to feel that he or she is a failure.

Recognizing Troublesome Behaviors

As their dementia gets worse, patients often develop troublesome behaviors. They may wander away from home and become lost, start fires by leaving food burning on the stove, or bully children in the family. They may become violent, attacking their caregivers or others. Some patients hoard useless objects, rifle through drawers and cabinets, or open every unlocked door in the house.

This fascination with doors, drawers, and cabinets can mean the end of personal privacy for every member of the household. According to Pat North, director of an Alzheimer's facility in Virginia, the urge to open doors is a common trait of dementia: "[Patients will] go through the halls, opening all the doors . . . searching, searching, searching, convinced that if they open the right door, on the other side it will all make sense."[56]

Other patients may develop a peculiar condition known as sundowner syndrome, or simply "sundowning." For reasons that no one understands, sundowners become more agitated and disoriented in the evenings. They may pace endlessly, see and hear things that aren't there, cry out repeatedly, or deliberately break things.

Sleep disturbances are also common. Some patients refuse to get into bed at night, sleeping instead in a chair, on a sofa, or even on the floor. Others wake in the middle of the night and wander through the house, often making it impossible for others to sleep.

Problem behaviors such as these can disrupt households, destroy families, and endanger the mental and physical health of all concerned. When the home situation becomes unmanageable, a doctor, psychologist, or social worker may recommend placing the patient in residential care.

Residential Care for Alzheimer's Victims

Once, the chief options for Alzheimer's care were nursing homes and state hospitals. Neither suited the needs of dementia patients especially well, however. Nursing homes were set up for people who were mentally intact but physically unable to care for themselves; the behavioral problems common to Alzheimer's disease could disrupt the quiet, hospital-like environment. State hospitals, on the other hand, cared for the mentally ill or mentally retarded, groups whose needs could be very different from those of people with Alzheimer's disease.

As awareness of Alzheimer's disease increased, so did the options for care. Today, there are several different types of Alzheimer's facilities, each with its advantages and disadvantages. They include assisted living facilities, life care communities, special Alzheimer wards in traditional nursing homes, and state-of-the-art dementia care units.

Assisted Living and Life Care

Assisted living facilities are often good choices for moderately impaired Alzheimer's victims because they provide care without completely altering the patient's life. Instead of a hospital room, the person has a pleasant apartment. Instead of being a patient, he or she is called a resident.

In the typical assisted living facility, residents eat in a communal dining room that often resembles a nice restaurant. They receive regular housekeeping services and personal assistance with grooming and hygiene. There are ample opportunities for socializing and engaging in a variety of interesting activities.

There is one drawback to even the best assisted living programs, however; sooner or later, the resident will have to move. As the disease progresses, he or she will need more care than as-

Assisted living facilities are often the best choice for moderately impaired Alzheimer's patients.

sisted living can provide. At that point, a nursing home or specialized Alzheimer's facility may be the best alternative.

However necessary a move might be, it creates problems for everyone involved. The family must inspect many facilities to find a suitable place. The patient must be uprooted from a familiar environment and placed among strangers.

Life care retirement communities attempt to solve this problem before it arises. They offer different levels of service to suit changing needs. A person might start out in a private apartment, move to assisted living when he or she needs additional help with daily routines, and then move to a nursing home for round-the-clock care. Though patients still move, they do so within familiar surroundings.

According to Dr. Jonathan M. Evans of the Mayo Clinic, a life care facility "offers people with Alzheimer's disease the chance to live in one place for the rest of their lives. Loved ones have the peace of mind that no matter what future care is needed, it's available, if not in the same room, then at least within the same complex."[57]

Nursing Homes and Alzheimer's Care Units

Unlike assisted living and life care, nursing homes are hospital-like facilities for people who are physically frail or ill but mentally intact. They are not set up to deal with the opposite condition—people who are mentally demented but physically vigorous. For this reason, some traditional nursing homes do not take dementia patients. Those that do often set aside a special ward for people with Alzheimer's disease and other dementias.

Some of these wards are special only in the sense that they are set aside for Alzheimer's patients. Many of them are not equipped, and their staffs are not trained, to deal with Alzheimer's-related behavioral problems. Patients who become troublesome may simply be sedated or restrained.

A traditional nursing home would probably not be the first choice for physically vigorous Alzheimer's patients. However, it may be the only reasonable choice for patients who also have chronic medical problems. For example, someone with diabetes, kidney disease, or heart disease may need the kind of medical care that nursing homes are equipped to provide.

For physically active patients, specialized Alzheimer's care facilities are often the best choice. Unlike nursing homes, they are planned, built, and operated with the needs of dementia patients in mind. The layout of the facility is set up to minimize problem behaviors. For example, circular halls and outdoor wandering paths allow patients freedom of movement without the danger that they will become lost. Potentially dangerous tools or utensils are kept safely out of the way. Doors to supply rooms and other off-limits areas are securely locked. Common areas are free of clutter to stumble over, bric-a-brac to break, and heavy objects to throw or use as weapons.

In this environment, odd behaviors can be tolerated as long as they do not injure anyone or unduly disrupt other patients. Wanderers can wander to their heart's content; hoarders can hoard. Even sundowning and sleeplessness are less disruptive in a care facility than in a private home.

Despite all these measures, even the best-designed facility occasionally receives a patient that the staff cannot handle. Patients who are prone to violence or who consistently intimidate other patients may have to be sent to a state mental hospital, where the staff is accustomed to dealing with the most difficult cases.

Many different care options are available for Alzheimer's patients, and families should choose a facility that best matches the needs of an individual patient.

The Challenge of Living with Alzheimer's Disease

Regardless of where a patient receives care, living with the relentless decline of Alzheimer's is difficult for caregivers and patients alike because the disease affects the person's sense of self. Some patients in the earliest stages of the disease can describe their feelings and sensations; in the later stages, though, this becomes impossible. And the patient loses the power to reflect on his or her condition.

Early-stage statements are usually brief and often make use of telling images to convey feelings. For example, Elizabeth P. once said that Alzheimer's was "like a hole in my brain . . . it opens up, and memories fall into it, and are gone forever."[58]

A patient named Charles described the symptoms and feelings that led him to seek medical help: "I knew something was wrong. I could feel myself getting uptight over little things. People thought I knew things [at work] that I . . . couldn't remember. The counselor said it was stress. I thought it was something else, something terrible. I was scared."[59]

Effective caregivers acknowledge the feelings of patients like Elizabeth and Charles but do not dwell on them. They focus instead on the day-to-day needs of the patient, coping with problems as they arise and finding small satisfactions wherever they can. Until science finds a preventative or a cure for Alzheimer's disease, that is the best anyone can hope to do.

Chapter 6

Looking to the Future

BY THE BEGINNING of the twenty-first century, Alzheimer's research was pursuing important new findings about the disease. Studies aimed at preventing, delaying, or stopping Alzheimer's opened the possibility of new and effective treatments.

A postdoctoral student tests tissue cell cultures in one of the labs at the University of Kentucky's Chandler Medical Center.

According to researchers, these developments hold great promise for the future. Alzheimer's researcher Marilyn Albert summed up the prospects by referring to her own career: "When I started working in this area in the early 1980s, I never thought that I would see effective treatments for this disease in my lifetime. . . . Now I assume I will, in the not-too-distant future. It's remarkable."[60]

Alzheimer's and Mild Cognitive Impairment

In March 1999, the National Institute on Aging announced a major study of a newly described condition known as mild cognitive impairment, or MCI. According to an article from UPI Science News, MCI is "a condition that is somewhere between normal age-related forgetfulness and the memory loss, confusion, and the mental decline that marks the onset of Alzheimer's dementia."[61]

People with MCI show memory difficulties similar to those of early Alzheimer's disease, but without other symptoms such as language difficulties and loss of judgment. Dr. Ronald C. Petersen, lead researcher of the new study, explained the difference: "With MCI you have a memory disorder only and other cognitive functions—attention span, problem solving, language, personality—are relatively preserved and normal. . . . In [Alzheimer's] memory is impaired but these other functions start to deteriorate as well."[62]

Mild cognitive impairment is a major risk factor for Alzheimer's disease. Ten to 15 percent of people develop Alzheimer's within a year of their diagnosis with MCI. This compares to about 1 percent of the general population. Many researchers believe that if they could find a way to stop MCI from turning into full-blown Alzheimer's, they could slow the rate of cognitive decline or maybe stop it completely.

Even if a connection between MCI and Alzheimer's were established, however, putting that knowledge to practical use would depend on early diagnosis. It is a simple fact of medicine that diseases are easier to treat in their earliest stages, and there is nothing in the research to indicate that Alzheimer's will be an exception to this general rule.

Advances in Diagnosis

Early diagnosis of Alzheimer's could uncover treatment possibilities that do not exist today. According to researcher Dr. Gregory T. Golden, even a fairly short delay could help millions of people because doing so would push the onset of symptoms beyond the lifespan of many people who would otherwise be stricken with the disease. Golden says, "the National Institute on Aging estimates that if we could delay the onset of symptoms of Alzheimer's disease by five years we could cut the number of cases in this country by 50 percent. If you delay onset by ten years, it would cut the number of cases by 75 percent within a generation."[63]

In order for early detection to work, though, scientists have to identify the disease before symptoms become obvious by developing accurate testing procedures to detect the abnormalities that cause the symptoms. For example, currently, researchers are working on laboratory tests that would detect abnormal amyloid or tau proteins in spinal fluid, blood, or urine. Such tests would indicate the presence of plaques or tangles in the brain.

Another important area of diagnostic research is imaging technology. Computer-aided scans allow scientists to observe the

This researcher is conducting image analysis, one of the most recent technological advances available for Alzheimer's disease research.

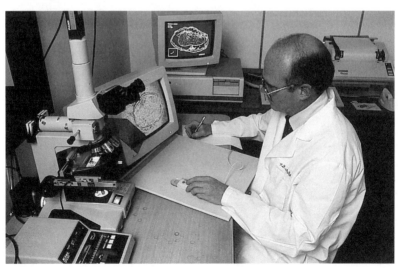

brain at work. Such scans of people doing memory tasks have already yielded significant results. Normal subjects exhibit a certain pattern of organized activity in the memory centers of the brain. In people with Alzheimer's, however, that pattern breaks down. Activity in the memory centers becomes scrambled and weak. If this process can be linked to Alzheimer's disease, doctors would be able to compare a patient's scan to the normal ones and detect Alzheimer's in its earliest stages.

The scans are valuable not only for diagnosis. They could also play a critical role in evaluating possible treatments. By studying how substances such as vitamin E, estrogen, and anti-inflammatory drugs affect the brain, researchers can better determine their effectiveness in preventing or delaying the onset of symptoms.

The Search for an Alzheimer's Vaccine

Prevention was also the goal of one of the most exciting research projects of the late 1990s: the attempt to develop an Alzheimer's vaccine. Until 1999, the prospect of such a vaccine seemed remote. Then in July of that year, researchers at the drug company Elan announced that they had developed a vaccine that stops plaque formation in the brains of mice.

According to a report by CNN,

> Young mice genetically engineered to develop Alzheimer's disease were immunized with [the vaccine] before they developed the brain plaques. Thirteen months later, the immunized mice showed no signs of disease.
>
> In a second experiment, mature mice showing signs of Alzheimer's brain damage were treated with [the vaccine] for seven months. Researchers found that during that time, plaque formation was not only halted, but reduced.[64]

These results caused science journalist Steve Sternberg to speculate that "Someday, a vaccine to guard against Alzheimer's disease may be as common as a flu shot."[65] The scientists who conducted the experiments share Sternberg's enthusiasm, but they also caution that even a successful vaccine might not be the answer to preventing Alzheimer's disease entirely. These re-

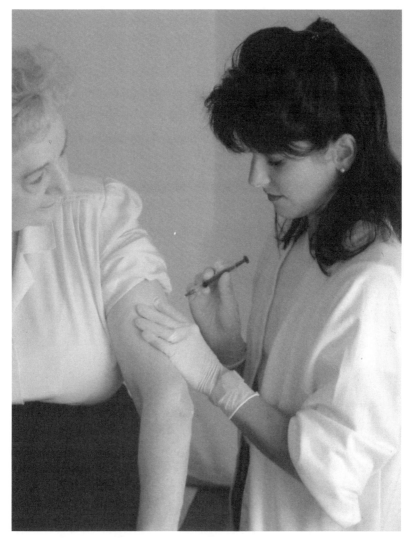

Currently there is no vaccine for Alzheimer's, but many researchers feel they are very close to developing one.

searchers are still not sure that amyloid plaques are the cause of Alzheimer's. If there is another force at work, they contend, eliminating the plaques will not prevent the disease.

This does not mean that an anti-amyloid vaccine would have no value, however. Scientists do know that plaques are a symptom of Alzheimer's and that they damage the brain. Eliminating them should therefore slow the progress of the disease or perhaps make its symptoms milder. In addition, it would have a research benefit. A vaccine that eliminated plaques without stopping the disease would conclusively demonstrate that amyloid deposits are not the cause of Alzheimer's. In doing so, it would also resolve the long-standing debate about the relative importance of amyloid plaques and tau tangles.

For decades, doctors have argued over which symptom (plaques or tangles) caused the most trouble in the Alzheimer's brain. As Steve Sternberg explains, "If the vaccine eliminates [amyloid plaques] and people still develop dementia, the failure will indicate that tau is a bigger problem than [scientists] thought."[66] That fact alone would have major implications for the future of Alzheimer's research.

Advances in Genetic Research

In addition to vaccine research, genetic studies have also focused on amyloid. In late 1999, scientists found two enzymes responsible for cutting, or breaking down, normal amyloid proteins into the toxic fragments that form plaques in the Alzheimer's brain. Named beta-secretase and gamma-secretase, these enzymes belong to a class of brain chemicals known as protease enzymes. These are normal chemicals the body uses to break down proteins after they have done their job.

In Alzheimer's disease, the secretase enzymes malfunction. Just how or why this happens is unclear, but the result leaves protein debris in the brain, which then forms plaques. According to an article in *Science News,* "After beta-secretase snips away one end of [the normal amyloid] . . . gamma-secretase . . . slices a chunk off the other end to produce [the plaque-causing debris]."[67]

The discovery of these enzymes might one day lead to drugs that could stop plaque formation by inhibiting secretase. Though scientists are excited about the possibilities, many of them caution that finding an inhibitor and developing it into a drug that is safe for human use is a long way off.

Dr. Martin Citron, head of the team that found beta-secretase, estimated "that it would be several years before a potential drug

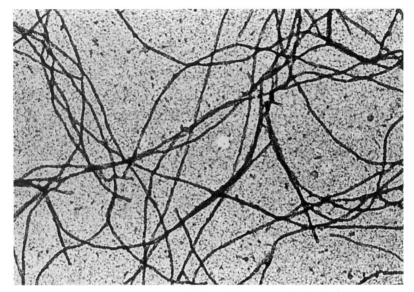

An Alzheimer's vaccine would resolve the debate over which symptom, plaques (shown here) or tangles, causes the most trouble in Alzheimer's patients.

was found and tested sufficiently in the laboratory and in animals [to be ready for] . . . tests with people."[68]

Alzheimer's Disease and Brain Research

In addition to genetic research and other studies that focus directly on Alzheimer's, general studies of the brain have also produced exciting results. Until the end of the twentieth century, scientists believed that nerve cells could not regenerate, or grow. They thought that once lost through age, injury, or any other cause, these cells were gone forever, meaning that damage to the brain or nervous system was permanent.

In 1999, however, researchers found convincing scientific evidence that this was not true. Science journalists Dianne Hales and Robert E. Hales, biologists at Princeton University discovered that

> Monkey brains constantly produce thousands of new neurons, which travel to the cerebral cortex, the center of higher intellectual functions. . . . Earlier studies had [shown] . . . brain

growth in mice placed in stimulating environments and an increase in neurons in canaries when they learn new songs. The same process occurs in humans.[69]

The Princeton results were confirmed by yet another study, this one at the University of Tennessee. Researchers there succeeded in growing human brain cells in a culture, or nutrient solution. According to Hales and Hales, this work "may be a crucial step toward the development of techniques to use a patient's own . . . cells to regenerate neurons and repair an injured or diseased brain."[70] If cells can grow in a dish, say the scientists, they can also grow in the human body.

A Race Against Time

Given the level of knowledge about the brain, practical applications of this research may be decades away. In the meantime, those who deal with Alzheimer's disease have to accept the hard fact that afflicted people cannot be restored to normal function, and hope for the immediate future lies in preventing Alzheimer's or stopping its progression in the mildest stages.

Alzheimer's research is often referred to as a "race against time" because of the millions who will be afflicted if a cure is not found.

Without effective treatment, the number of Americans afflicted with Alzheimer's disease is expected to rise from about 4 million in 2000 to 14 million by 2050. People who work with Alzheimer's disease know those numbers all too well. As Maureen Reagan wrote in her article about former president Ronald Reagan's battle with Alzheimer's disease, "We are in a race against time for all of us."[71] It is a race that those in the forefront of Alzheimer's treatment and research are determined to win.

Notes

Introduction: The Thief of Memory

1. Muriel R. Gillick, *Tangled Minds: Understanding Alzheimer's Disease and Other Dementias.* New York: Penguin, 1999, p. 96.

Chapter 1: A History of Alzheimer's Disease

2. Gillick, *Tangled Minds*, p. 75.
3. Quoted in Gillick, *Tangled Minds*, p. 75.
4. Gillick, *Tangled Minds*, p. 75.
5. Quoted in Jeremy Laurance, "The First Woman with Alzheimer's," *Independent*, April 5, 1997, p. 8.
6. Gillick, *Tangled Minds*, p. 81.
7. Gillick, *Tangled Minds*, p. 82.
8. Joseph Rogers, *Candle and Darkness: Current Research in Alzheimer's Disease.* Chicago: BasicBooks, 1998, p. 31.
9. Gillick, *Tangled Minds*, p. 116.
10. Quoted in Daniel A. Pollen, *Hannah's Heirs: The Quest for the Genetic Origins of Alzheimer's Disease.* 2nd ed. New York: Oxford University Press, 1996, p. 77.

Chapter 2: The Search for Answers

11. Rebecca Rupp, *Committed to Memory: How We Remember and Why We Forget.* New York: Crown, 1998, p. 9.
12. Rupp, *Committed to Memory*, p. 24.
13. Rogers, *Candle and Darkness*, pp. 41–42.
14. Quoted in University of Pennsylvania Health System, "Penn Scientists Identify Major New Alzheimer's Disease Pathology," July 26, 1997. www.med.upenn.edu/news/News_Releases/july97/alzheimer.html.
15. Quoted in Wade Roush, "Alzheimer's: New Lesion Found in Diseased Brains," *Science*, July 10, 1997. www.mad-cow.org/~tom/Alzheimer_july.html.
16. National Institute of Neurological Disorders and Stroke (NINDS), "Huntington's Disease: Hope Through Research,"

1999. www.ninds.nih.gov/patients/Disorder/HUNTINGT/ HDHTR.HTM.

17. Quoted in NINDS, "Huntington's Disease: Hope Through Research."
18. Pollen, *Hannah's Heirs*, p. 119.
19. Rogers, *Candle and Darkness*, p. 83.
20. Quoted in Pollen, *Hannah's Heirs*, pp. 140–41.
21. Rogers, *Candle and Darkness*, p. 84.
22. Pollen, *Hannah's Heirs*, p. 263.

Chapter 3: Diagnosis
23. Maureen Reagan, "My Father's Battle with Alzheimer's: What I've Learned from President Reagan and His Struggle," *Newsweek,* January 31, 2000. http://newsweek.com/ nw-srv/printed/us/so/a54601-2000jan23.htm.
24. Rogers, *Candle and Darkness*, p. 96.
25. Nancy L. Mace and Peter V. Rabins, *The 36-Hour Day: A Family Guide to Caring for Persons with Alzheimer Disease, Related Dementing Illnesses, and Memory Loss in Later Life,* 3rd. ed. Baltimore, MD: Johns Hopkins University Press, 1999, p. 14.
26. Gillick, *Tangled Minds*, p. 15.
27. Jeffrey W. Hull, *Parents' Common Sense Encyclopedia,* 1996–2000. www.drhull.com/practice/.
28. Gillick, *Tangled Minds*, p. 21.

Chapter 4: Treatment
29. Mayo Health Oasis, "Drugs to Combat Alzheimer's Disease," 1999. www.mayohealth.org/mayo/9911/htm.
30. Geoffrey Cowley, "Alzheimer's: Unlocking the Mystery," *Newsweek,* January 31, 2000. www.newsweek.com/.
31. Gillick, *Tangled Minds*, pp. 58–59.
32. Vincent W. Delagarza, "New Drugs for Alzheimer's Disease," *American Family Physician,* 1998. www.aafp.org/afp/98100lap/ delagarz.html.
33. Quoted in Mayo Health Oasis, "Estrogen to Treat Alzheimer's Disease: New Role for ERT," 1998. www.mayohealth.org/ mayo/9804/htm/ert_alz.htm.
34. Merritt McKinney, "Hormone Therapy Does Not Slow Alz-

heimer's," *Reuter's Health,* February 22, 2000. www.alzheimers. com/news/20000222-3347.html.

35. Mayo Health Oasis, "Estrogen to Treat Alzheimer's Disease."
36. Delagarza, "New Drugs for Alzheimer's Disease."
37. Mace and Rabins, *The 36-Hour Day,* p. 99.
38. Mace and Rabins, *The 36-Hour Day,* p. 162.
39. Quoted in Rupp, *Committed to Memory,* p. 230.
40. Rupp, *Committed to Memory,* p. 232.
41. Kate O'Rourke, "The Way We Were: Reminiscence Therapy Programs Keep Alzheimer's Patients Conversing," *Baltimore Jewish Times,* August 28, 1998, p. 70.
42. Quoted in O'Rourke, "The Way We Were," p. 70.
43. Jason J. Meixsell, "Basic Remotivation Therapy." www6. bcity.com/remotivation/.
44. Meixwell, "Basic Remotivation Therapy."
45. Naomi Feil, *The Validation Breakthrough: Simple Techniques for Communicating with People with "Alzheimer's-Type Dementia."* Baltimore, MD: Health Professions Press, 1993, p. 130.
46. Fiel, *The Validation Breakthrough,* p. 254.
47. Fiel, *The Validation Breakthrough,* p. 256.
48. Fiel, *The Validation Breakthrough,* pp. 49–50.
49. Naomi Feil, "VIEWPOINTS: Communicating with the Confused Elderly Patient," *Geriatrics,* March 1984. www. vfvalidation.org/article1.html.
50. Feil, "VIEWPOINTS: Communicating with the Confused Elderly Patient."

Chapter 5: The Human Equation

51. Interview with the author, Clearlake, California, November 1996.
52. Susan McClelland, "Hidden Heartbreak," *Macleans Online,* January 17, 2000. www.macleans.ca/pub-doc/2000/01/17/ Cover/29133.html.
53. Mace and Rabins, *The 36-Hour Day,* p. 212.
54. Quoted in Fahizah Alim, "Quiet Despair," *Sacramento Bee,* November 4, 1998, p. E-1.
55. Alzheimers.com, "The Amazing Power of Support Groups," 2000. www.alzheimers.com/health_library/coping/coping_ 12_support.html.

56. Quoted in Tamara Jones, "Calming the Confusion of Alzheimer's, *Washington Post,* February 20, 1997, p. M1.
57. Mayo Health Oasis, "Alzheimer's: Choosing a Care Facility," 1999. www.mayohealth.org/mayo/9810/htm/alz.htm.
58. Interview with the author, Apple Valley, California, June 1993.
59. Quoted in Mace and Rabins, *The 36-Hour Day,* p. 8.

Chapter 6: Looking to the Future

60. Quoted in Steve Sternberg, "A Culprit Identified in Alzheimer's Disease: Frustration Turns to Optimism That a Remedy Is Closer," *USA Today,* October 25, 1999, p. 8D.
61. UPI Science News, "Study to Seek Way to Halt Alzheimer's," March 15, 1999.
62. Quoted in Electric Library, "Mild Cognitive Impairment Can Be Distinguished from AD," *Geriatrics,* May 1, 1999. www. elibrary. com/.
63. Quoted in *Saturday Evening Post,* "Diagnosing Alzheimer's Disease," January/February 2000, p. 38.
64. CNN Online, "Test of Alzheimer's Vaccine in Mice Shows Promise," July 7, 1999. http://cnn.com/HEALTH/9907/07/ alzheimers.vaccine.02/.
65. Sternberg, "A Culprit Identified in Alzheimer's Disease," p. 8D.
66. Sternberg, "A Culprit Identified in Alzheimer's Disease," p. 8D.
67. J. Travis, "Enzyme Offers Promise of Alzheimer's Drugs," *Science News Online,* November 6, 1999. www.sciencenews.org/ sn_arc99/11_6_99/fob5.htm.
68. Quoted in Gina Kolata, "Scientists Find Enzyme Linked to Alzheimer's," *New York Times,* October 22, 1999. www. pebio.com/ab/BioBeat/breakthru.html#bk51.
69. Dianne Hales and Robert E. Hales, "The Brain's Power to Heal," *Parade Magazine,* November 21, 1999, p. 10.
70. Hales and Hales, "The Brain's Power to Heal," p. 12.
71. Reagan, "My Father's Battle with Alzheimer's."

Glossary

autopsy: Examination of a body after death.

biopsy: Removal and examination of tissue from a living subject.

cell: The smallest structural unit of an organism that is capable of independent functioning.

cerebral cortex: The outer portion of the brain, in which thought processes take place.

chromosome: A strand that carries genes and transmits hereditary information.

clinical trial: A study that tests the value and safety of medical treatments on human beings.

cognitive abilities: The higher mental functions, such as memory, learning, judgment, and reasoning.

diagnosis: The act of determining the nature and cause of a disease or injury.

differential diagnosis: A working list of possibilities that a doctor uses in the beginning of the diagnostic process.

disorientation: A state of confusion regarding place, time, or personal identity.

DNA (deoxyribonucleic acid): A nucleic acid that carries the genetic information, or "code," for building a living thing.

electron microscope: A microscope that uses a stream of electrons instead of light to magnify an image.

enzyme: A substance that starts a biochemical process without being changed by that process.

familial: Occurring among members of a family, usually by heredity.

gene: The basic unit of heredity; a section of DNA that codes for a particular trait.

genetic susceptibility: Being more likely than the average person to develop a disease as a result of heredity.

impairment: A diminished ability or function.

neurologist: A doctor who specializes in treating disorders of the nervous system.

neurotransmitter: A chemical messenger that carries information from one nerve cell to another.

paranoia: Extreme, irrational suspiciousness or feelings of persecution.

predisposition: Susceptibility or inclination toward a particular condition or disease.

prognosis: A prediction of the probable course and outcome of a disease.

psychosis: A mental disorder characterized by irrationality and loss of contact with reality.

psychotropic: Drugs that alter behavior or perception.

respite: A short break or time away.

risk factors: Attributes that increase a person's likelihood of developing a particular disease.

senility: Term meaning "old," once used to describe dementia in elderly people.

side effect: An unintended result of taking a drug.

sundowning: Agitation and unsettled behavior that regularly occurs in late afternoon or early evening.

toxin: A poisonous substance produced by a living organism.

Organizations to Contact

Alzheimer's Association
919 N. Michigan Ave., Suite 1000
Chicago, IL 60611-1676
(800) 272-3900
Internet: www.alz.org

This organization provides educational materials and public awareness programs. Local chapters in many communities have established support groups for Alzheimer's patients and their families.

Alzheimer's Disease Education and Referral Center (ADEAR)
P.O. Box 8250
Silver Springs, MD 20907-8250
(301) 495-3311
Internet: www.alzheimers.org

A branch of the National Institute on Aging, ADEAR distributes information and free materials for the general public, patients and their families, and health care professionals.

Children of Aging Parents
1609 Woodbourne Rd., Suite 302-A
Levittown, PA 19057
(215) 945-6900
Internet: www.caregide.net

Provides education and referrals for adult children who care for a parent stricken by Alzheimer's disease.

National Family Caregiver Association
10605 Concord St., Suite 501
Kensington, MD 20895-2504

(301) 942-6430
Internet: www.nfcacares.org

The association provides information and assistance for people who care for Alzheimer's patients at home.

Safe Return
P.O. Box 9307
St. Louis, MO 63117-0307
(888) 572-8566

Safe Return provides identification bracelets for Alzheimer's victims. These bracelets show the name of the person and his or her caregiver, along with the toll-free phone number of Safe Return. The information aids in returning Alzheimer's patients to their homes in the event they become lost.

For Further Reading

Books

Susan Gold, *Alzheimer's Disease*. Parsippany, NJ: Silver Burdett Press, 1996. Case histories of real people with Alzheimer's disease are interwoven with an overview of symptoms, diagnosis, and treatment.

Elaine Landau, *Alzheimer's Disease*. New York: Franklin Watts, 1996. A discussion of Alzheimer's, with particular emphasis on how it affects the patient's family. Offers suggestions for coping and caregiving.

Diana McGowin, *Living in the Labyrinth: A Personal Journey Through the Maze of Alzheimer's*. New York: Dell, 1994. A personal account of what it feels like to have Alzheimer's. Written when the author was in the early stages of the disease.

Joseph Rogers, *Candle and Darkness: Current Research in Alzheimer's Disease*. Chicago: BasicBooks, 1998. A good introduction to Alzheimer's research by a professional who knows how to write for the general reader.

Beth Wilkinson, *Coping When a Grandparent Has Alzheimer's Disease*. New York: Rosen, 1995. Guidelines for young people facing Alzheimer's disease in a grandparent. Gives suggestions for coping with stress and grief.

Websites
Alzheimer Web
www.alzweb.org
This website has a mixture of scientific, organizational, and personal information related to Alzheimer's disease. Includes a "tour" of the brain and a series of graphics showing brain structure.
Alzheimers.com
www.alzheimers.com/news/
This website has information and links on all topics related to Alzheimer's disease.

Alzheimer's Organizations: Directory of Aging Sites
www.aoa.dhhs.gov/aoa/webres/alz-corg.htm
This directory website is an excellent starting point for Alzheimer's information on the web.

Works Consulted

Books

Naomi Feil, *The Validation Breakthrough: Simple Techniques for Communicating with People with "Alzheimer's-Type Dementia."* Baltimore, MD: Health Professions Press, 1993. The founder of validation therapy explains its principles and possible uses. Case histories help to illustrate and humanize the various points.

Muriel R. Gillick, *Tangled Minds: Understanding Alzheimer's Disease and Other Dementias.* New York: Penguin, 1999. Excellent overview of the history, science, and personal impact of Alzheimer's disease.

Nancy L. Mace and Peter V. Rabins, *The 36-Hour Day: A Family Guide to Caring for Persons with Alzheimer Disease, Related Dementing Illnesses, and Memory Loss in Later Life.* 3rd ed. Baltimore, MD: Johns Hopkins University Press, 1999. A comprehensive guide to caring for Alzheimer's patients and dealing with their problem behaviors.

Daniel A. Pollen, *Hannah's Heirs: The Quest for the Genetic Origins of Alzheimer's Disease.* 2nd ed. New York: Oxford University Press, 1996. An account of one of the most important scientific quests of the twentieth century.

Rebecca Rupp, *Committed to Memory: How We Remember and Why We Forget.* New York: Crown, 1998. A readable study of the working of memory.

Periodicals

Fahizah Alim, "Quiet Despair," *Sacramento Bee,* November 4, 1998.

Dianne Hales and Robert E. Hales, "The Brain's Power to Heal," *Parade Magazine,* November 21, 1999.

Tamara Jones, "Calming the Confusion of Alzheimer's," *Washington Post,* February 20, 1997.

Jeremy Laurance, "The First Woman with Alzheimer's," *Independent,* April 5, 1997.

Kate O'Rourke, "The Way We Were: Reminiscence Therapy Programs Keep Alzheimer's Patients Conversing." *Baltimore Jewish Times*, August 28, 1998.

Saturday Evening Post, "Diagnosing Alzheimer's Disease," January/February 2000.

Steve Sternberg, "A Culprit Identified in Alzheimer's Disease. Frustration Turns to Optimism That a Remedy Is Closer," *USA Today*, October 25, 1999.

UPI Science News, "Study to Seek Way to Halt Alzheimer's," March 15, 1999.

Internet Sources

Alzheimers.com, "The Amazing Power of Support Groups," 2000. www.alzheimers.com/health_library/coping/coping_12_support.html.

————, "Many Do Not Recognize Early Signs of Alzheimer's Disease," *Reuter's Health*, December 24, 1999. www. alzheimers. com/news/19991224-2480.html.

CNN Online, "Test of Alzheimer's Vaccine in Mice Shows Promise," July 7, 1999. http://cnn.com/HEALTH/9907/07/alzheimers.vaccine.02/.

Geoffrey Cowley, "Alzheimer's: Unlocking the Mystery," *Newsweek*, January 31, 2000. www.newsweek.com/.

Vincent W. Delagarza, "New Drugs for Alzheimer's Disease," *American Family Physician*, 1998. www.aafp.org/afp/981001ap/delagarz.html.

Electric Library, "Mild Cognitive Impairment Can Be Distinguished from AD," *Geriatrics*, May 1, 1999. www.elibrary.com/.

Marilyn Elias, "Brain Scans Search for Alzheimer's." *USA Today*, May 16, 2000. www.usatoday.com/life/health/seniors/alzheim/lhsal035.htm.

Naomi Feil, "VIEWPOINTS: Communicating with the Confused Elderly Patient," *Geriatrics*, March 1984. www.vfvalidation. org/article1.html.

Jeffrey W. Hull, *Parents' Common Sense Encyclopedia*, 1996–2000. www.drhull.com/practice/.

Gina Kolata, "Scientists Find Enzyme Linked to Alzheimer's," *New York Times*, October 22, 1999. www.pebio.com/ab/BioBeat/breakthru.html#bk51.

Mayo Health Oasis, "Alzheimer's: Choosing a Care Facility," 1999. www.mayohealth.org/mayo/9810/htm/alz.htm.

————, "Drugs to Combat Alzheimer's Disease," 1999. www.mayohealth.org/mayo/9911/htm/alzquestions.htm.

————, "Estrogen to Treat Alzheimer's Disease: New Role for ERT," 1998. www.mayohealth.org/mayo/9804/htm/ert_alz.htm.

Susan McClelland, "Hidden Heartbreak," *Macleans Online,* January 17, 2000. www.macleans.ca/pub-doc/2000/01/17/Cover/29133.shtml.

Merritt McKinney, "Hormone Therapy Does Not Slow Alzheimer's," *Reuter's Health,* February 22, 2000. www.alzheimers.com/news/20000222-3347.html.

Jason J. Meixsell, "Basic Remotivation Therapy." www6.bcity.com/remotivation/.

National Institute of Neurological Disorders and Stroke, "Huntington's Disease: Hope Through Research," 1999. www.ninds.nih.gov/patients/Disorder/HUNTINGT/HDHTR.HTM.

Maureen Reagan, "My Father's Battle with Alzheimer's: What I've Learned from President Reagan and His Struggle," *Newsweek,* January 31, 2000. http://newsweek.com/nw-srv/printed/us/so/a54601-2000jan23.htm.

Wade Roush, "Alzheimer's: New Lesion Found in Diseased Brains," *Science,* July 10, 1997. www.mad-cow.org/~tom/Alzheimer_july.html.

J. Travis, "Enzyme Offers Promise of Alzheimer's Drugs," *Science News Online,* November 6, 1999. www.sciencenews.org/sn_arc99/11_6_99/fob5.htm.

University of Pennsylvania Health System, "Another Piece Fits in the Alzheimer's Puzzle," 1997. http://health.upenn.edu/ADC/.

————,"Penn Scientists Identify Major New Alzheimer's Disease Pathology," July 26, 1997. www.med.upenn.edu/news/News_Releases/july97/alzheimer.htm.

Index

brain, 91–92
diagnostic, 87–88
genetic, 90–91
residential care, 80–83
risk factors, 44–46, 86
Rogers, Joseph, 19, 30–31, 36, 37,
45–46
Roses, Allen, 39
Roth, Martin, 23
routine, 76
Rubin, David, 64
Rupp, Rebecca, 27, 28, 64

selegeline, 60
senile dementia. *See* dementia
senility, 12, 13–14
sleep disturbances, 79
spinal tap, 50
state hospitals, 80, 83
Sternberb, Steve, 88, 90
St. George-Hyslop, Peter, 38
sundowner syndrome, 79
support groups, 79
symptoms, recognizing, 43–44

tacrine (Cognex), 33, 55–57

Tangled Minds (Gillick), 48
tangles, 16, 23, 30–31, 90
task-related difficulties, 44
tau, 30, 39
therapy. *See* psychological therapies
36-Hour Day, The (Mace and
Rabins), 46, 64
thyroid deficiencies, 49–50
Tomlinson, Bernard, 23
treatment, 55–70
drugs for, 55–60
general health care and, 61–62
preventatives and, 59–60
promising new, 59–60
psychological therapies and,
62–64
Trojanowski, John, 32

vaccine, 88–90
validation therapy, 66–69
Van Zandt, William, 55–56
vitamin deficiencies, 49
vitamin E, 60

wills, 74
Wong, Caine, 36

Picture Credits

Cover photo: © Tony Stone/John Livzey
© Bill Aaron/Photo Researchers, Inc., 78
© Henny Allis/Science Photo Library, 29
AP Photo/Beth A. Keiser, 92
AP Photo/Julia Malakie, 81
AP Photo/Breck Smither, 85
AP/World Wide Photos, 10, 17, 38, 40, 56
Archive Photos, 13
© Lester V. Bergman/Corbis, 27, 36
© Bettmann/Corbis, 42
© Oscar Burriel/Latin Stock/Science Photo Library, 58
© Corbis, 15
© Jim Cummins/FPG International, 9, 34
© Simon Fraser/MRC Unit, Newcastle General Hospital/Science
    Photo Library, 18, 22
© Evan Johnson/Impact Visuals, 45, 63, 83
© Kevin Laubacher/FPG International, 43
© Mike Malyszko/FPG International, 47
© Ursula Markus/Photo Researchers, Inc., 53, 68, 74, 75
© Stephanie Maze/Corbis, 77
© Richard Nowitz/Photo Researchers, Inc., 67
© Alfred Pasieka/Science Photo Library, 31
© Photo Researchers, Inc., 71, 89
© Dr. Huntington Potter/Science Photo Library, 91
© Terry Qing/FPG International, 49, 51
© Chip Simons/FPG International, 20
© SIU/Photo Researchers, Inc., 87
© Telegraph Colour Library/FPG International, 61
© Charles D. Winters/Photo Researchers, Inc., 59

About the Author

Linda Jacobs Altman has written many books for young people. She specializes in history and social issues, having written on topics such as the Holocaust, slavery, and hate groups. Her books for Lucent include biographies of Cesar Chavez and Simon Wiesenthal.

Altman and her husband live in the small town of Clearlake, California, with four dogs, four cats, and two cockatiels. They have two grown sons and three grandchildren. When not writing, she enjoys reading, singing in a choir, and surfing the Net.